First published in the United States of America in 2021.

Copyright © 2021 Carline Anglade-Cole. All rights reserved.

No part of this book may be reproduced in any form or by any electronic or mechanical means, including information storage and retrieval systems, without written permission from the author, except for the use of brief quotations in a book review.

Hardback: 978-1-7352569-4-8

Paperback: 978-1-7352569-5-5

Ebook: 978-1-7352569-6-2

Audiobook: 978-1-7352569-7-9

This book was produced with the assistance of a remarkable writer and editor named Laura Gale.

Feel free to contact Laura at laura.gale@lauraiswriting.com to help you develop your own book project.

Book cover design by Rick Thayne.

Rick and I have worked together for nearly 20 years on numerous and successful direct-response projects. He's a master of his craft. You can contact him at rickthaynedesign@gmail.com to help you create a kick-butt design.

My apologies in advance for omissions, misspellings and perceived factual inaccuracies. I hate typos but they seem to love me.

## ALSO BY CARLINE ANGLADE-COLE

*"My Life as a 50+ Year-Old White Male: How a Mixed-Race Woman Stumbled Into Direct-Response Copywriting and Succeeded!"*

2021 Bronze Award from the Nonfiction Authors Association and 2021 Bronze Award from the Independent Publishers Book Awards. And an Amazon Best Seller!

Available at https://bit.ly/mylifebyCarline

<u>Copywriting Training Manuals:</u>

*How to Write Kick-Butt Copy: Straight Talk from a Million-Dollar Copywriter*

*Anatomy of a Kick-Butt Control: How to Create a Winning Promo from Start to Finish!*

*Which One Won? How to Write Kick-Butt Headlines and Boost Response*

*How to Write FASTER Copy... Cut Down Your Writing Time By More Than 50%... and DOUBLE Your Income!*

*How to Write Magalogs, Tabloids and Other Monster Promos!*

Available at www.carlinecole.com

# YOUR COPY SUCKS — YOU DON'T!

60 KICK-BUTT LESSONS ON COPYWRITING... BUSINESS... AND LIFE!

CARLINE ANGLADE-COLE

# KUDOS
## FOR CARLINE ANGLADE-COLE

### "I'm a huge fan!"

"Carline, I want to subscribe to your email list! And I'd buy a collection of your ads in a heartbeat! Thanks again for all your excellent work on the Clayton Makepeace Tribute. The video you posted today looks great. All the best!"

GARY BENCIVENGA, LEGENDARY COPYWRITER

### "One of the best!"

"Carline Anglade-Cole is a "human dynamo" in the copywriting world — incredibly energetic and productive; one of the best copywriters working today; a superb teacher of copywriting; and a true direct marketing guru.

Plus, she's one of the nicest people I know, inside or outside of the advertising universe.

On top of all of that, she sure writes great books!"

BOB BLY, A-LIST COPYWRITER AND AUTHOR OF OVER 100 BOOKS

### "Carline is a one of a kind writer!"

"Boy does Carline take direct-response writing to another level!

Love it when she creates a sales promo for us. She's open to suggestions and works closely with us to create a killer control.

I would highly, HIGHLY recommend her!"

VIC DI CRISCIO, PRESIDENT, NORDIC CLINICAL

### "A Copywriting High Profit MEGASTAR!"

"Carline generated more sales and profits for one of my companies than every other copywriter I hired COMBINED. I've never met anybody who can create high profit advertising so consistently. Almost everything she touches turns to gold."

CALEB O'DOWD, MARKETING COACH & CONSULTANT.

### "A Life FORCE!"

"Carline Anglade-Cole is a brilliant and groundbreaking copywriter. She's a smart and savvy business builder. She brings humor and positivity to everything she does. There's really no other way to say it... she is an absolute life FORCE!"

KATIE YEAKLE, CEO, AWAI

### "Carline is an amazing copywriter, mentor, and friend!"

"Carline has written countless successful health and supplement promos and generously shares her knowledge to help up-and-coming copywriters. Her 'crazy' headlines, positive attitude, and background story are an inspiration to many, including me. Any time you spend learning about copywriting from Carline will be amongst the most valuable — and enjoyable — time you spend!"

KIM KRAUSE SCHWALM, A-LIST COPYWRITER AND COPY MENTOR

### "Carline is the real deal!"

"As a copywriter, Carline understands the "art of persuasion." She is smart, well-read and has an insatiable curiosity about life. She also has a distinct ability to turn ideas into compelling copy. Plus, she's a joy to work with!"

DENISE FORD, CONFERENCE AND EVENTS DIRECTOR, AWAI

### "An inspiration!"

"Carline is one of a kind. She blows me away with her energy, generosity and bold action. She inspires me every time we talk!"

LAURA GALE, GHOSTWRITER AND EDITOR

### "You are a rare gem!"

"Carline – you are the epitome of a GENEROUS friend... MOTIVATING mentor... EMPOWERING role model... and CREATIVE coach!

You know I could keep going with LOTS more to describe you! But my point is – I'm grateful to have you in my life. You OOZE with energy and passion for life... love... and business.

And you don't hold back from sharing your wisdom with those who listen. I'd be a fool to take for granted your unfailing support and guidance in both my personal life and copywriting career!"

MARCELLA ALLISON, COPYWRITER AND FOUNDER, MENTORESS COLLECTIVE

### "You united the copywriting community for an amazing cause!"

"Wow Carline, you're on fire these days, congratulations! Your book is doing very well and I LOVED the Clayton Tribute event you put together — it was the best thing to happen for our community in quite a while."

PAM FOSTER, COPYWRITER, AWAI

**"I jump at the chance to work with Carline!"**

"Working with and knowing Carline Anglade-Cole is always an absolute pleasure. If she says YES to a project, you know it's going to be the best. She will put her full heart and soul in it.

This excellence is evident in her copy, her books, working with students and relationships with clients. I will always jump at the chance to work with Carline because of how she lifts me up with her joyous spirit."

JADE TRUEBLOOD, AWAI DIRECTOR OF TRAINING

**"Proud to be Carline's Copy Cub!"**

"Hi Carline — I'm still pinching myself — I'll be processing that class in my mind for weeks.

Honestly... all I can think is how grateful I am! I know what a huge deal it is to have the opportunity to work on a project like this with you... to have A-list graphic designer Rob Davis doing the artwork... and having Rick Popowitz on the chat! Unreal.

I worked for years with the opportunity-seeker/sweepstakes guys... and I always wanted to work with the 'real' copywriters and crews. So I can't thank you enough — I still have a lot to learn — but I'm goin' for it!"

SHAWN PHILLIPS, STUDENT OF CARLINE'S C.R.A.Z.Y COPY SYSTEM LIVE MENTORING SHOW

### "Received my first writing sample! Thanks Carline!"

"I just wanted to say that my day went from zero to a hundred, from gloomy to sunny, from apathetic to motivated... just WOW. I'm beyond grateful for the critique today and for all the other days filled with fun, energy and gold copy gems.

I just emailed all my relatives in Lithuania that Carline thought that my cover test was worthy! I'm beyond ecstatic! Thank you for such an awesome experience and an opportunity to touch the genius marketing and copywriting mind."

RAMUNE BLAZEVIC, STUDENT OF CARLINE'S C.R.A.Z.Y COPY SYSTEM LIVE MENTORING SHOW

### "Thank you for your giving spirit!"

"Hi Carline! Koman ou ye?

So excited to find out that you were of Haitian descent! Wanted to say WOW — what an amazing presentation you gave today at the Copy Accelerator seminar! Your copy examples really got the wheels turning in my mind — thank you!

I love your energy, your creativity, and your generosity in sharing with those who are coming behind you. I just picked up a copy of your book on Amazon. Can't wait to read it!

Thank you again!"

REBEKAH CHALKEY, COPYSTAR READER

**"Success in business... family... and life!"**

Carline is the definition of a woman who is a successful, published author and talented copywriter with numerous winning packages for multiple companies. But what is extra special and something I admire about Carline is that she has accomplished all this while keeping her faith and family a priority.

She is also paying it forward by mentoring the next generation of copywriters. She really is one-of-a-kind and has been great to work with."

ANNETTE PAYNE, OWNER, MEASURABLE RESULTS, II

**"A BIG THANKS for introducing me to the copywriting world!"**

"I am consistently BLOWN AWAY from what I learn from you! True friends are like diamonds... rare and hard to find. Your friendship is one of my prized possessions! Thank you for sharing your light with me! I GLOW when I'm with you!

And you inspire me to KEEP turning my goals into a reality!"

CYNTHIA HILL, COPYWRITER & CONSULTANT

### "Who writes not one – but TWO books during a pandemic? My mom – that's who!"

"My mom had a dream of writing her book — *My Life as a 50+ Year-Old White Male* — but she had no idea where that dream would take her.

She had no idea she'd become an Amazon best-seller and a 2X award-winning author! Or that she would get a self-published book into most of the Barnes and Noble locations across the country.

And she had no idea she'd do it AGAIN — just a year later and during the pandemic!

This time she writes *Your Copy Sucks — You Don't!* — her second book that's on its way to becoming an even BIGGER success!

Way to go Mom. You continue to inspire me and so many others. Love you!"

MILAN COLE DE HER, DAUGHTER #1,
COPYWRITER, COPYMILL MARKETING

## "Carline does it AGAIN!"

*Your Copy Sucks – You Don't!* is as insightful, honest, educational and funny as Carline's first book, *My Life as a 50+ Year-Old White Male*. But this time – we get a small peek into the 60 (or more!) lessons she learned that got her to where she is now. Let's hope there are #3 and #4 books in the works for more pearls of wisdom!

I've worked for Carline and have the privilege to be her friend – and I can say without hesitation that I've seen her use all these lessons in her life. She's also helped many others to benefit from these lessons too.

I encourage everyone to read this book (as well as her first book!). You will tap into the honest and hilariously funny mind of a wonderfully successful copywriter, wife, mother, friend and overall great human being."

MIRIAM SACCOMANI, DESIGN CONSULTANT
& FRIEND

**"You get straight talk from the MOMBOSS!"**

"That's what I tell copy cubs to expect on Carline's C.R.A.Z.Y Copy System LIVE Mentoring Show!

That's because "MOMBOSS" delivers the goods when she teaches aspiring copywriters how to write KICK-BUTT... A-Level... WINNING copy! I love seeing her "keepin' it real" and honest with our members!

OK – so I might sound biased – but there really is no other mentor like her! It's a joy working as her producer and co-host each week — and I just try to soak up as much of her CRAZY as I can!

My Mom & Boss is simply Da Bomb!"

TIARA M. COLE, DIRECT-RESPONSE COPYWRITER & GRAPHIC DESIGNER AND PRODUCER/CO-HOST OF CARLINE'S C.R.A.Z.Y COPY SYSTEM LIVE MENTORING SHOW

# CONTENTS

Dedication — xxv
Foreword — xxix
Introduction — xxxiii

**Lesson #1** — 1
*Tell yourself you feel good even if you don't. Your brain won't know you're lying.*

**Lesson #2** — 3
*Be a parent and not a peer.*

**Lesson #3** — 6
*You married your mate for a reason. If you don't know what it is before your wedding day — you're sure as heck gonna find out afterwards!*

**Lesson #4** — 9
*People in pain often lash out. Bite your tongue and don't retaliate.*

**Lesson #5** — 12
*Retire when you hate what you're doing. Even if it's at 40 — figure something else out.*

**Lesson #6** — 15
*Fire a client who disrespects or belittles you.*

**Lesson #7** — 18
*Tell your grandkids you love them more than your own children.*

**Lesson #8** — 20
*Your family are the people you really love and who love you back.*

**Lesson #9** — 22
*Stop blaming everything on your dysfunctional childhood. That was out of your control. But your adulthood is in your hands.*

**Lesson #10** — 24
*Buy your own flowers. They're not going to be any more beautiful coming from someone else.*

**Lesson #11** — 27
*Tell your mentors "Thank you". Show your appreciation by doing something very nice for them.*

Lesson #12  31
*Don't be stupid with your money. It can go faster than it came.*

Lesson #13  33
*That check is not ALL yours.*

Lesson #14  36
*Wear your special clothes and good jewelry every day — even to Walmart. Being alive and healthy is enough of an occasion.*

Lesson #15  39
*A good bra can make you look five pounds lighter. My favorite is the Natori Yogi Sports Bra.*

Lesson #16  42
*Your kids won't remember big family events before age 7 — so save Disney World until it counts.*

Lesson #17  44
*Don't make your kids your entire life. You really DO want them to grow up and move out.*

Lesson #18  46
*If you give a friend $20 and you never see him again, it was worth it.*

Lesson #19  48
*Don't confuse "principle" with "pettiness".*

Lesson #20  50
*I like me. If you don't — that's OK. Your loss.*

Lesson #21  52
*Hate the act, not the person.*

Lesson #22  54
*The day you give birth, open a "Therapy Fund". Your kids can use it to fix all the stuff you screw up while you raise them.*

Lesson #23  56
*There's always 10 things you'll hate about your mate. If you swap for another mate, that one will have 10 things you'll hate too. Might as well stick with what you know.*

Lesson #24  58
*The only person you can change is YOU. And even that's hard.*

Lesson #25  60
*Exercise is therapy. Running keeps me from going insane.*

Lesson #26  63
*Don't sign non-compete agreements. They protect the business but keep you in chains.*

Lesson #27     65
*Black people DO go to therapists — but they're called "girlfriends".*

Lesson #28     68
*When I look fat, I slap the heck out of the mirror and then waddle away!*

Lesson #29     71
*If you want to be a writer, well dang it, you gotta write!*

Lesson #30     74
*Be afraid — and do it anyway!*

Lesson #31     77
*It's good to have a moral compass. Mine is the Bible.*

Lesson #32     79
*Getting lost is how I discover new places and new friends. Unfortunately, I can't find them again.*

Lesson #33     81
*End an email, letter or note with "I love you" or other kind words.*

Lesson #34     83
*Your copy sucks — you don't!*

Lesson #35     86
*Protect your "me" time. If your pitcher is empty, you can't fill your cups.*

Lesson #36     88
*Pray. And when you're done, pray again. Praise Jah!*

Lesson #37     91
*Give freely. Give in secret. Give intentionally. Just give!*

Lesson #38     94
*Be a mentor without the title.*

Lesson #39     98
*Create a theme for each new year — and be true to it.*

Lesson #40     101
*Using profanity doesn't make you cool, big or bad. It just gives you a potty mouth.*

Lesson #41     103
*Travel reminds me how insignificant I am to the planet.*

Lesson #42     106
*Give a BIG tip for a little purchase.*

Lesson #43     109
*Don't be ashamed of where you came from. Use your past to launch your future.*

Lesson #44    111
*Showing humility takes courage.*

Lesson #45    114
*If you give me a gift that says "Assembly Required" — you are not my friend.*

Lesson #46    116
*It's only easy when you know how.*

Lesson #47    119
*After a trial, you can either be better or bitter.*

Lesson #48    121
*Don't hate your body parts. They're doing the best they can with what you feed them.*

Lesson #49    124
*Compliment generously. Criticize stingily — unless it's copy crits.*

Lesson #50    127
*I love my kids but I NEED my sanity.*

Lesson #51    130
*Show up early and you're two-thirds of the way to reaching your goal.*

Lesson #52    132
*An open hand receives more than a closed fist.*

Lesson #53    134
*Make people better off in ways they desire — and are willing to pay for.*

Lesson #54    136
*Write like you talk. I believe this is the #1 reason I'm a successful copywriter.*

Lesson #55    139
*Use your words wisely. They can hurt more than bullets.*

Lesson #56    142
*Ask yourself, "What would a great _____ do? (example: copywriter, mom, wife, friend). Then DO it!*

Lesson #57    144
*Do not come to my funeral. You are not invited. Have a "fun-eral" instead and enjoy the moments we shared.*

Lesson #58    146
*Treat your friends like a Board of Directors.*

Lesson #59    148
*A story can reach the heart and open the wallet.*

| | |
|---|---:|
| Lesson #60 | 150 |
| *I am not Superwoman. I just play one in life. Sometimes I really do need help.* | |
| Surprise! | 152 |
| Lesson #61 | 153 |
| *A handshake agreement is more binding to honest people than any lawyer-drawn contract.* | |
| Lesson #62 | 156 |
| *Put your pride aside and test, Test, TEST!* | |
| Lesson #63 | 158 |
| *Movement beats meditation.* | |
| A Special Gift For YOU! | 161 |
| A Blatant Attempt to Market and Self-Promote! | 167 |
| Give Me 60 Seconds... | 168 |
| Get A Daily Boost... | 169 |
| Let Me Take You On A Journey... | 170 |

*To my teachers and students in life.
I am thankful for every lesson learned —
whether acquired the easy or the hard way.*

# DEDICATION

Dang! If I had known I was going to write a second book — I wouldn't have put all the good stuff in the first one!

After all, my first book, *My Life as a 50+ Year-Old White Male: How a Mixed-Race Woman Stumbled Into Direct-Response Copywriting and Succeeded!* was like my first-born child. I had no idea what I was doing but I knew I wanted to do it!

So I just gave it my all and just hoped everything would be OK.

And boy was it ever! *My Life...* won 2 awards by the Nonfiction Authors Association and the Independent Publishers Book Awards. And it also became an Amazon Best Seller! Not too shabby for a rookie!

But now, I'm on baby #2 — and this experience was so different. I'm more comfortable and relaxed. I expected bumps along the way. I didn't sweat it. I went with the flow and relied on experience to carry me through the tough times. And this baby — similar to my own baby #2 — was a real joy to give birth to.

Since I have 4 children — could this mean there's a book #3 and #4 in my future? Who knows?

Along the way of this journey to create *Your Copy Sucks — You Don't! 60 Kick-Butt Lessons On Copywriting... Business... and Life!* — I maintained the same core of cheerleaders and critics: The people I can count on for encouragement and support — and also to tell me the raw truth — whether I want to hear it or not.

So I dedicate this book to my true friends. The women and men who keep me on the right path physically, mentally and spiritually.

If I tried to name everyone, I fear the risk of leaving someone out. And that would just be awful. So you know this book is dedicated to you — if you have ever...

... gotten a phone call from me in the middle of the night to help with a crisis.

... laughed with me so hard, we accidentally farted out loud (or peed just a little in our big girl panties).

... cracked me upside the head with a stone-cold truth.

... shared clothes — including underwear — because we didn't have time to do laundry.

... shed tears over bad decisions made by our children/mates/loved ones.

... taken an impromptu trip with me to save my sanity.

... showed up on my doorstep unexpected, uninvited — at the absolute perfect time.

... stayed up late to keep me company on the phone or in person — in a hospital lobby or parking lot... in a parked car at a Blockbuster's... or right outside the Intensive Care Unit awaiting test results.

... showed up with wine — knowing that you would be drinking most of it because I can't handle my liquor.

... or said — just about every time we see or talk to each

other, "Hello my friend, Carline!" — with a big smile in your voice!

If you see yourself in this list — then you are my true friend. And I love you.

* * *

A very special thank you to my editor Laura Gale. When I called Laura and said "Hey — I have an idea for another book" — without hesitation, she said, "I'm in!"

This is our second collaboration and I honestly would still be working on my first book if Laura hadn't kept me on track... helped organize my crazy thoughts... and supported my vision. I deeply appreciate and respect you Laura Gale.

* * *

This book evolved through decades of lessons learned and taught from my family. They are my ultimate Petri dish in the experiment of life. So, a great big, fat, juicy kiss to my husband Micarleo "Mickey" Cole... my four children Milan Cole De Her, Tiara Cole, Jael Cole and Chadam Cole... my grandsons Dallas De Her, Carson De Her, Maverick De Her and Colton De Her... my son-in-law Ethan De Her... and my mom — my #1 teacher, Michelle Anglade.

* * *

Ultimate thanks and praise belong to the Almighty God, Jehovah. www.jw.org

## FOREWORD
### BY MARCELLA ALLISON

If you've ever been fortunate enough to receive an email from Carline Anglade-Cole that begins with, "You know I love you, right?" then you have received some much-needed "schooling" as only Carline can deliver it.

As a multiple award-winning million-dollar international copywriter and mentor, Carline wants nothing more than to see you succeed, even at the risk of saying what is uncomfortable or difficult to hear. This is an extraordinary gift and one that has had a huge impact on my career and my life.

Between these pages, you'll discover for yourself the "schooling" that can help you improve your marriage, better parent your children, deepen your faith, build a successful business and become a better listener and friend, just to name a few.

The first time I met Carline Anglade-Cole, I was a struggling copywriter. There were very few successful women at the highest level in the copywriting industry at the time and Carline was one of them. I began to study her copy and to watch every presentation I could find so that I could learn from her. As I grew in my own career, I got to know Carline personally and to benefit from her generosity firsthand.

I will never forget the time I hosted a private dinner for female copywriters, marketers, and creatives and I invited Carline to attend. Carline had just been asked to give the keynote talk at one of our largest industry events and she shared that she was thinking of saying no. At the time she was in incredibly high demand as one of the top performing copywriters in the world *and* she was busy running her business and taking care of her family.

At that dinner I told Carline how much her mentoring and generosity had impacted me and others in the industry. Carline came up to me afterwards and said, "You know, I listened to you tonight and I realized you're right. This isn't about me. This is about paying it forward to others. I'm going to say yes." And she's continued to say yes to mentoring others and paying it forward over and over again ever since.

Carline is a founding sponsor of the *Mentoress Collective*, an organization dedicated to helping women go as fierce and as far in business and life as they desire. Over the years, Carline has continued to donate her time, money, and mentoring to hundreds of women in the collective. She contributed a wisdom-filled chapter to our award-winning book, *Why Didn't Anyone Tell Me This Sh\*t Before*. And she shared her own book, *My Life as a 50+ Year-Old White Male: How a Mixed-Race Woman Stumbled Into Direct-Response Copywriting and Succeeded!* with the collective in one of our most popular *Literary Salons* ever.

Today Carline gives away million-dollar copywriting tips and expertise for free to both men and women on her popular Carline Cole YouTube Channel. She mentors and trains the next generation of copywriters in her *C.R.A.Z.Y Copy System Live Mentoring Show*. And she continues to inspire and motivate thousands of men and women in her CopyStar email community.

But Carline's mentoring doesn't stop with copywriting... not by a long shot.

Her loving advice and mentoring has not only helped me to improve my copywriting, but to grow my business, become a better parent, make wiser choices with my money, and deepen my faith. And now she is sharing that same wisdom with you in this book. With nearly every lesson I read in *Your Copy Sucks — You Don't! 60 Kick-Butt Lessons on Copywriting... Business... and Life!* I could point to a time when Carline first shared that wisdom with me and to the difference it has made in my own life.

Carline has inspired me to take bigger risks and to attempt things I thought were beyond my ability, simply by watching her take big leaps in her own career. She is never one to rest on her laurels but always finds a way to push herself to meet new challenges.

When I do take those risks, Carline is always there with a text message, a call, a word of encouragement. She shows up for the people in her life with all her love, energy and wisdom — just as she is showing up for you in this treasure-trove of advice.

Carline will tell you the truth when you need to hear it and with your permission, not from a place of judgement but from a place of love and support. As you read these pages, open your heart, close your mouth and listen and I promise that you'll be a better person for it.

She also will make you laugh harder than you've ever laughed before. I've learned it's dangerous to read Carline's books with a cup of coffee because I inevitably end up accidentally snorting it!

If you are a person of faith, you'll also love how Carline

incorporates her faith into her everyday life. She's taught me a lot about how to rely on my spirituality during difficult times without ever getting preachy.

You'll also receive some much-needed schooling on how *not* to screw up with money. Carline is always pushing me to balance generosity with the need to make a profit. And she's taught me that I cannot help others if I do not take care of myself first.

She's even inspired me to make some important changes in my own health and to make better choices when it comes to eating and exercising.

I like to tease Carline that she accomplishes more before 6 a.m. than most folks get done all day. There's nothing better than waking up to an early morning text from Carline with a much-needed bit of inspiration, motivation, or "You Go Gurrl-ll!" to start your day.

So take the time to read these kick-butt lessons and absorb their power. Give yourself the gift of Carline pushing you, encouraging you and gently nudging you to be the very best you can be. I know you will discover — as I have — that when you've got Carline in your corner cheering you on, anything is possible.

Marcella Allison
Author, A-list Copywriter, and Founder, *Mentoress Collective*

# INTRODUCTION

Age 35　　　Today!

If you ask me how old I am right now — I would not hesitate to say "35!"

I feel like I'm 35. I have the energy of a 35 year-old. And I've been told — many times — I look 35.

But the truth is, I've got a daughter who's 35 — and she's not even my oldest kid!

I've been married for over 38 years.

I have over 34 years of experience as a direct-response copywriter and marketer.

And I've got clothes in my closet that are waaayy over 35 years old.

But right now — as I write this book, I'm 60.

I don't know how the heck that happened — but it did!

I experienced A LOT of great memories and experiences as I racked up those 60 years.

I also learned some powerful lessons you might find useful.

And I've discovered that even some of my biggest "mistakes" didn't turn out to be so bad after all!

So I decided to write this book — to share with you 60 kick-butt lessons I learned before I turned the big 6-0.

Now, these lessons are not in any particular order. There's no #1 lesson, no #1 answer. They are all powerful lessons that taught me a lot — and you can benefit from them — should you choose to use them.

Hopefully these lessons will give you insight... clarity... and even a "heads up" on what you can look forward to in life — if you haven't reached 60 yet.

Let me tell you this right now: These 60 lessons can make or break your life. Do you hear me? Follow them and you have a proven shortcut to success. Ignore them at your own peril.

Aw shucks, I'm just kidding!

That's just the copywriter coming out in me. It's my need to create drama, intrigue and flair!

The truth is: What you're about to discover might not seem earth-shattering at all. But I'm willing to bet they'll give you an "AHA" moment... clarity... confidence... and even confirmation that you're heading down the right path!

I will never claim they are the final words on anything. But they are my words ... my truths... my observations... and my successes.

In fact, the book title, *Your Copy Sucks — You Don't!* are words my copy cubs hear right before I tear into their copy to give them crits. But I realize those words are also a confirmation about life. Stuff happens and it doesn't mean you're a bad person because it happens to you.

Before I sat down to write these lessons, I hadn't thought about them in a specific order. I knew I had general attitudes and beliefs that I based my life on — but when I took the time to write them all down — I realized, Wow! They turned out to be really good guidelines for my life!

These lessons helped shape my career as a direct-response copywriter — who rose through the ranks of a male-dominated profession and became a 3X award-winning, million-dollar copywriter and author.

That's just a fancy-schmancy way of saying, "Dang Girl, You're GOOD!"

They're lessons I learned while raising my four children — Milan, Tiara, Jael and Chadam — with my husband of 38 years, Micarleo "Mickey" Cole. And those kids turned out pretty amazing, each in their own eclectic way.

And they're lessons I learned about life, friendships, triumphs, spirituality, pain and most importantly, love.

These lessons helped me justify taking up space on this earth. They helped me build a pretty awesome and remarkable life. And they're made for sharing. I believe they will help you to find your way if you need direction... to impart wisdom if you seek guidance... and to make you smile if you're feeling drained or lacking motivation.

Use my 60 lessons as a gift. I don't claim to know all the answers. I sure ain't no psychologist, sociologist or any other type of 'ologist'!

But I do know a heck of a lot about motivation, persuasion, joy, kindness, friendship and love. I share with you my discoveries — not to say they're perfect — but to show you one version of a flawed, yet successful path.

Walk in it or not. The choice is yours.

But the gift is mine to give.

And this is what I want to share with you now...

Carline Anglade-Cole

## LESSON #1

TELL YOURSELF YOU FEEL GOOD EVEN IF YOU DON'T. YOUR BRAIN WON'T KNOW YOU'RE LYING.

When I was a kid, I used to ask an older gentleman who lived in my building the same question: "How are you feeling today, sir?" And each time he said the same thing: "If I felt any better, I'd be twins!"

Now I could tell he was in some pain. But his disposition was so positive that it left an impression on me. *If I felt any better, I'd be twins.*

As I got older and studied how the brain behaves, I realized your brain does not differentiate between how you say you feel and how you really feel. If you say it, your brain believes it. Your brain doesn't know you're joking — so it takes what you say as gospel truth.

Yeah, some days you may get up and feel lousy. Maybe you're sick or something hurts.

But guess what? You got up. You took a breath. Many people did not have that option today. So you're already ahead of the game!

I believe that it's OK if I feel bad — but my point is not to dwell on it because your brain is going to follow suit with the words that come out of your mouth.

So on the days you don't feel great — fake it 'til you make it!

You do this all the time with people anyway. For example: You may be in a bad mood or don't feel great and someone asks, "How are you doing today?" Immediately you say "Fine, thanks!" and then you tell 'em, "Have a great day!" At that instant, you gave your brain a jolt of positivity! So, just because you're not feeling it right at that moment doesn't mean it's not valuable to say it.

Now, I'm not telling you to lie to yourself when things are really not OK. But I've learned that most irritations and bad moods can clear up on their own if you just feed your brain with positive thoughts.

Every day is a new opportunity and you can start each day by telling yourself that it's going to be a good one. That's what I do! Every morning before I leave my bedroom, I read an affirmation from my *Examining The Scriptures Daily* booklet and I meditate on something I'm thankful for. It takes just a few minutes and it resets my brain for positivity throughout the day.

Set yourself up for a successful day. Identify something you're grateful for. Let it bring a smile to your face. It will help you feel good — even if you've got plenty of reasons to feel bad.

## LESSON #2
### BE A PARENT AND NOT A PEER.

When my kids were little they'd get mad at me for saying "no" and they'd yell, "You're not my friend!"

Well, guess what kiddo? I don't want to be your friend. Being your friend is not my job and I've got better friends than you anyway!

Look —we love our kids and want to have a great relationship with them. But as a parent, your responsibility is to *parent*. Your goal is not to be your child's friend. OK?

A friend and a parent are on different levels. Your child has lots of friends but they only have one of you. Don't forsake your parenting responsibilities just to be their friend.

Your role is to teach your children. They don't know squat and they'll get on your nerves. But you have the power to help them grow into amazing adults. But you do that as a parent — not a peer.

You can't be a parent and a friend to your kids at the same time. Those roles conflict.

I'm not saying you can't hang out and do fun stuff with your kids when they're young. You can do that without relinquishing the role of parent. You can facilitate a lot of fun but you also have to be the one to say NO when needed!

Parents have more authority and influence than friends. But I've seen many parents forsake their role so their kids will like them. And I have often flat out asked them "Why are you treating your 10-year old as your equal? He/she is a kid!"

Friends are equals. Your child is not your equal until they become an adult. And even then — you still have the upper hand!

Your kids will have dozens of friends in life. And that's great — that's how it should be! But you, as the parent, need to be the stabilizing force in their life. Your kid needs to know they have someone to go to. They need to feel safe, protected and loved — and that's your job.

Now, I don't mean that you act like a dictator all the time.

Communication is key. I told my kids they could talk to me about anything. "You can tell me whatever you want. I will listen to you. I may not agree with you but we can talk about anything." I wanted them to know that as their mother, I would listen to them, I would believe them and I would back them.

Building that relationship was very important because if there was ever a conflict at school or if something strange happened — my kids knew that I would hear them out and I trusted them.

If someone said "Your daughter did this or said that" — I could say, "Well that's interesting because that's not really her personality. But let me check into it." And then I would figure out what was going on. Fortunately, my husband is very good at putting missing pieces together. So as a team, we usually got to the bottom of the issue.

My kids will tell you that I talked them to death. By the time they were teenagers, they were like, "Please Mom! Stop talking! No more!" But they knew I was there for them and ready to talk! But when they invited friends over, I was not trying to hang out with them. I was not their friend and I didn't act like it.

Now my kids are adults in their thirties and we have become friends. I choose to be around them. I look forward to the phone calls and I enjoy their company. I'm still their mom but we can have adult conversations. We can agree to disagree and that's OK with me.

It's wonderful to have that type of relationship now as adults but not when they're still children. It's not fair to your kids. So be a parent and not a peer.

## LESSON #3

YOU MARRIED YOUR MATE FOR A REASON. IF YOU DON'T KNOW WHAT IT IS BEFORE YOUR WEDDING DAY — YOU'RE SURE AS HECK GONNA FIND OUT AFTERWARDS!

I know the #1 reason I married my husband. And I remember the exact moment when it happened.

It was nothing earth-shattering — and it was a little embarrassing — but it was a "moment".

We spent a Saturday afternoon running errands, playing games and hanging out with friends. I was exhausted. So when we came back to his parents' house to watch T.V., I fell asleep on his shoulder.

It must have been some good sleep because I *drooled* on him.

When I woke up, I saw the drool spot and I was so embarrassed. Now, let me tell you, Mickey Cole is a comedian and will make fun of you at a drop of a hat. But he just gently took my head, laid it back on his shoulder and stroked my hair.

At that moment I experienced a feeling that I had never gotten from anyone else. I felt so safe and protected. I just loved that feeling and I wanted to be with the person who made me feel that way.

So, yes, I love and respect him and all that stuff but the

REAL reason I married Mickey Cole is because he makes me feel safe and protected. And he continued to do so during our courtship.

We've been married for 38 years and nobody has ever made me feel so safe and secure. And I get that feeling every time I put my head on his shoulder when we hug.

I've discovered that because I feel so safe with him — it allows me to go CRAZY and attempt all sorts of adventures! For example...

The day I asked Mick, "Do you think I should quit my job and try to become a freelance copywriter?" He said "Go for it. Whatever happens, I got you."

It's not like we were swimming in money. He was a firefighter and we definitely had bills! But he wanted me to be happy. And if taking the risk to venture off into the copywriting unknown was going to do that — then he would do whatever it took to make sure our family was OK.

He's my home base. And home base is always covered when Mickey Cole is around!

I know that many people struggle with an unsupportive spouse who discourages you from pursuing your dreams. That's why I'm thankful for my guy.

So on the rare occasions he doesn't agree with one of my crazy ideas — I gotta force myself to stop and listen, because, dang, there must be something he sees that I don't!

Now let me tell you this: If you blindfold me and spin me around in my own house, I will be lost when you take that blindfold off. My husband, on the other hand, has a keen sense — and I mean a *keen* sense — of direction and insight. Not only can he find a place — but he can walk into a room and he can tell if something's "off".

He'll say, "Why is that chair there? It wasn't there yesterday. Who's been in here?" He sees that kind of stuff a lot. I am clueless. CLUE-LESS, I tell ya! I wouldn't notice a giant sign on a door that says "AX MURDERER INSIDE." I would just stroll right in.

Fortunately for me, my husband notices the things I don't. He keeps me safe. And I love that.

So take the time to ask yourself "Why do I want to marry this person?" That means you've got to be honest with yourself about what you need or desire.

Set yourself up to have a happy marriage. Make sure you know what you need and decide if that person can provide it for you. And vice versa.

The truth will manifest itself — and it's better if it's before the "I do" than after.

## LESSON #4

### PEOPLE IN PAIN OFTEN LASH OUT. BITE YOUR TONGUE AND DON'T RETALIATE.

Pain — whether it's mental or physical — can make you say and do things completely out of character. Pain makes you angry and scared — sometimes at the same time. Pain reminds you that you lack control of your own body. And that sucks.

That's why people can lash out and say very hurtful things.

One time a very close friend said, "You get on my nerves with your Polly-Anna attitude. Not everyone can be as perfect as you!" I came to her house to be encouraging, helpful and supportive. But at that moment, I wanted to punch her in the face and give her even more pain!

I didn't. But I REALLY wanted to.

So my lesson learned is this: It's easy to retaliate in self-defense. It takes control and courage to hold back.

When you realize the person is suffering and in pain, then you can pause and take the higher road. You can deflect those words because you know that comment is out of character for that person. You can think more about the real cause and not the immediate action. You can make an excuse for their rash comment and even forgive.

This is not to say you have to be a punching bag for them. Take your leave from abusive conversations. But you can acknowledge this is not normal behavior. And then find a way to let it go and not make matters worse.

Think about your history. Their good qualities. The value of the relationship. These are tools in your forgiveness arsenal to use.

See if you can find an opportunity to show empathy if not sympathy. If you can do that, you shift your brain into problem-solving instead of attack mode!

I learned this over and over again during the COVID-19 pandemic.

Everybody — I mean EVERYBODY — was going through stuff at the same time. Getting sick from this unexplainable disease... losing loved ones... job losses... and ISOLATION. One of those is enough to make you go crazy — but many of us were dealing with multiple issues at once.

I became very aware that people around me are dealing with a lot. So a comment like, "What do you know about losing your job — you still have YOURS" can be ignored or excused — instead of looking at it as an invitation for an argument.

If it's a passing comment, let it pass.

If somebody you don't know says something that's hurtful, you can blow it off. You can go, "OK! That's a good one, I haven't heard that one before." You can dismiss it much easier than if it's a close friend who starts attacking you.

The better you know the person, the more it will hurt you if they say something mean. Yet that's when you need to bite your tongue the most.

It's fine to say, "OK, thank you" and move on. Or you could say "I'm sorry you feel that way. How can I help?"

Responses like this are much more powerful than "Oh, yeah? You wanna know what I think about YOU?!"

## LESSON #4

I have an amazing friend named Miriam Saccomani. She has this remarkable ability to deflect. I mean, if you really want to offend her, you practically have to say, "Miriam, what I'm about to say is intentionally meant to offend you. Please take it that way!" LOL!

I've known her for over 17 years and I have seen her deflect the most unbelievable, unthoughtful comments. One day I just had to ask her how the heck she does it!

She just said, "If somebody says something to me that's negative, I think about it and see if there's some truth in the statement. And if there is, I thank them for bringing it to my attention. The rest, I'll dismiss. It's not worth getting upset over."

So make exceptions for people — especially if they are in pain. I hope people will do the same for me.

## LESSON #5

### RETIRE WHEN YOU HATE WHAT YOU'RE DOING. EVEN IF IT'S AT 40 — FIGURE SOMETHING ELSE OUT.

While I was working on this book, I sent out an email to my CopyStar readers with the subject line, "Announcing my retirement." Oh man — my inbox BLEW UP! My subscribers couldn't believe I was getting out of the biz — but I wasn't quitting copywriting.

No. You see, I retired years ago. I just didn't realize it until I was hanging out with some girlfriends and we started talking about retirement plans.

Some couldn't wait to quit their jobs to start doing what they REALLY wanted to do.

Many had plans for volunteer work... disaster relief projects... traveling... or flat out NOT doing ANYTHING anymore!

They were, in essence, fulfilling the definition of "retirement" according to the Oxford Dictionary:

"The action or fact of leaving one's job and ceasing to work... the time of life when one chooses to permanently leave the workforce behind."

Then I heard the question, "What about you Carline, what

do you plan to do when you retire?" And I thought, "Dang! I'm doing it now!"

I left Corporate America and hung out my copywriting shingles over 22 years ago. I was sick of my high-pressure 9-to-5 job. I was sick of not being in control of my time. I was sick of missing out on school trips with my kids. I was sick of the commute. And I was definitely sick of the day-to-day "politics" to get ahead!

I'm not sure — but can you tell I was SICK of it?

So I quit.

And while it took a few years to build up a freelance copywriting reputation and track record to give me a fantastic income...

... I had left the grind of Corporate America behind. I definitely "ceased working!" I mean, what I do now is not "work" — it's FUN!

I control my time — and do what I want when I want. I choose the people in my work life. I create value for my clients and my market. And I don't wake up dreading going to the office. In fact, many times my "office" is my comfy bed!

Now, you might be thinking, "Carline, I need insurance. I've got kids to feed. I need a job to pay the mortgage." And I totally get it. But I also believe you can get that by doing something that you actually enjoy.

You spend a third of your life working. Do you really want to hate nearly 30 years of your life?

You have to realize that you can do something different — something that doesn't feel like work anymore. Something that's FUN now — not later!

Let me tell you a story about my friend Lou. He talked about retirement like it was the Holy Grail. He planned to retire from his sales job at age 62. And he worked night and day to get in a financial position so he could enjoy his golden years.

He postponed family vacations. Worked on weekends. Spent little time with the family. Had no hobbies. His reasoning was, *"I'll do all that when I'm retired."*

For the 15 years I knew him — that's how Lou lived. And then he turned 62. A month later, he was dead.

He developed a sudden illness and died three and a half weeks after he retired. He did not get to do any of the things he had postponed until retirement. He didn't even receive a single pension check!

WOW. Talk about a powerful lesson learned — and a punch in the gut. Lou helped me realize that you can't wait until retirement to enjoy life. You gotta do it NOW.

Don't waste away a third of your life. Ask yourself: What value can I bring to a position and how do I go about finding a job that I actually like?

If you have a good intellect and good people skills, you've got leverage. If you can get along with people — you can get a job. The rest is stuff you can learn as you go.

Don't spend a third of your life treating work like a means to an end. If you don't like the job, it's not for you. Get out of it. You have to give yourself permission to do it — and to believe in yourself.

There's something else out there for you —so hurry up and "retire" so you can do what you love NOW!

## LESSON #6

### FIRE A CLIENT WHO DISRESPECTS OR BELITTLES YOU.

If you're a freelancer —and especially if you're a newbie — here's a powerful lesson I want you to know right now:

Your client does not own you. Your client does not dictate your work schedule. Your client does not get to treat you like a punching bag.

Your client is not your boss. You are limited-time partners with the goal to accomplish a specific task or project.

You are your own boss.

Many writers, especially young writers, feel they have to put up with disrespectful treatment from their clients. Maybe you don't think you have the same level of experience and you're still learning. Maybe you put up with their disrespectful behavior because you're afraid of getting fired. Or maybe you just think that's the way it is in the freelance field.

Well, my answer to that is: Heck no.

Even if you're a total rookie, there needs to be mutual respect in the relationship. And that respect has to start from Day One. You don't need to "pay dues" to earn respect.

If mutual respect doesn't exist — you're in a bad work environment. Is that what you really want? Didn't you become a freelancer to get out of the corporate crapola?

Now, I know sometimes things can get crazy on the job. Sometimes you're on a deadline and tempers can flare and tension can get high. People say things in the heat of the moment and then regret it later. Make allowances for that.

But what I'm talking about here is consistent disrespect.

If that client is unrealistic with expectations... if they are rude to you... if they make comments that you feel are inappropriate...

You cannot allow the paycheck to excuse the disrespectful relationship.

If you say to yourself, "Yep, he's arrogant, he's racist, and he's completely unreasonable — but I need the money so I'm going to put up with it"... STOP.

Don't do it. Stand up for yourself. Speak out.

When you stand up for yourself and do what you believe is right, you may be surprised. Often I've found the client didn't realize he was being a pain in the butt. You might get an apology and a better relationship going forward.

And if that client says, "If you don't like it, too bad," then at least you know what you're working with.

Don't work with jerks. Do not work with people who make you feel bad about yourself or who intentionally try to tear you down.

Have the guts to say to yourself, "I don't care if this person is my income. I deserve better than this."

You might want to find another client before firing this one — so you don't completely disrupt your income — but if a client is being disrespectful, belittling or even abusive, stand up for yourself.

Tell them: "This is not acceptable. I will not work in this type of environment. We can end this relationship today if necessary" — even if you don't have something else lined up yet. Be true to what you're saying and follow through.

My mentor, the legendary Master Copywriter Clayton Makepeace once gave my daughter #1 Milan a piece of valuable advice. Milan was working with a jerk of a client. However, she was making more money than she ever made in her career. But she hated her job. Here's what Clayton told her:

"Do not become hostage to a paycheck that may or may not be here tomorrow."

Those words gave Milan the guts and confidence to fire that client — and a month later — she landed an even BIGGER client and BIGGER paycheck!

But even better — when you stand up and speak out — it makes a world of difference for your self-respect and how the client views you. It shows the client — and even future clients — that you're not a pushover. You have rights and you deserve to be respected.

Like Milan experienced, when you get rid of that nastiness and negativity, usually something MUCH better surfaces. That's because you've made space for it. But if you keep holding on to that negativity, there's no room for something better to come along.

Lesson learned: Have the guts and self-respect to fire your client when necessary.

## LESSON #7

### TELL YOUR GRANDKIDS YOU LOVE THEM MORE THAN YOUR OWN CHILDREN.

The four most amazing moments in my life were giving birth to my four children. I absolutely love my kids and I love being their mom. I was dedicated to helping them grow to become decent human beings. That was my job as a mom — but man oh man — it was a lot of work!

Today I've got four grandsons — Dallas, Carson, Maverick and Colton — and I love being "Coco" — their grandmother. I get to do all the awesome fun things I did with my kids — but I don't have to deal with any of that hard work anymore!

If I call my daughter and say, "Hey, I want to come over and hang out with the boys," and she says, "OK but they're sick and throwing up right now," I say, "Ohhhh... I'll stop by next week instead!"

I don't have to deal with vomit or get bags under my eyes from staying up all night taking care of sick kids. That's a mother's job. I'm Coco! I get to give them 100% of my love and I can skip all that hard mothering stuff.

Been there. Done that.

I love having grandkids because I'm no longer the disciplinarian. Coco and C-Pop's house is their favorite place in the world! When they come over here, it's like Disney World — eat as much candy as you want and have as much fun as you can.

Now, I will discipline them if I have to — because I'm not going to have bratty grandkids —but their parents are doing a great job so I seldom have to step into that role.

My job is to be an awesome, amazing grandmother. So I tell my kids, "Don't mess up my job because you're not doing yours!"

My goal with my grandkids is for my daughter to use me as her ultimate weapon: "If you don't straighten up, you're not going to Coco and C-Pop's house". And that would be the worst punishment EVER for those amazing grandsons of mine!

And the reverse also works for me. If my grandsons are at my house and they're acting up, all I have to say is, "Do I need to call your mom to come pick you up?" And then I'll hear, "No, no, I'll be good, sorry!"

When my grandkids complain about me, I want them to say "Dang it! My grandmother is loving me to *death!*" LOL.

So that's why I tell my grandkids, "I love you guys way more than my kids." It just makes them feel so special. Because they know how much I love my own children!

## LESSON #8

YOUR FAMILY ARE THE PEOPLE YOU REALLY LOVE AND WHO LOVE YOU BACK.

Family are the people you would do anything for — and who in turn — would do anything for you.

It has nothing to do with your last name or your DNA.

Well... maybe not quite.

I've learned that blood is not thicker than water. Even if you have a good family relationship, the people who are really your family are the ones you love and the ones who love you back.

So many of my real family are not blood relatives.

However, I can't honestly say I will do ANYTHING for my family. I've learned to establish boundaries. Why?

Because there will be times when you need to cut relatives out of your life to save your sanity.

If you can help them, you do it the best you can. But you can't continue to the point of self-harm.

If they're on a bad course — don't support them just because they're your brother or sister or child or whatever the case may be.

If they're doing things you don't agree with or if they're being harmful or abusive — then you have to draw the line.

You don't owe them anything just because you're related.

If I can help the person from a distance, I will do the best I can. Maybe it's paying for rehab... finding a therapist... getting them food or a place to live — then OK. But I can't stay emotionally engaged to the point where I become a hot mess!

My family are the people that make me feel good... uplift me... encourage me... and have my back. They're the ones who have been in my kids' lives from Day One as their "aunts and uncles". And many are still very involved to this day. They are there for me as much as they can be. And I am there for them.

That is how I have learned to define family.

## LESSON #9

STOP BLAMING EVERYTHING ON YOUR DYSFUNCTIONAL CHILDHOOD. THAT WAS OUT OF YOUR CONTROL. BUT YOUR ADULTHOOD IS IN YOUR HANDS.

Letting go of your childhood is part of growing up. It's a part of owning yourself and releasing what doesn't serve you.

I know people who had horrific childhoods, yet you would never know it from talking with them. And I know people who had horrific childhoods — and that is *all* you hear about! They still talk about what their mother or father did or didn't do... even though they're over 60 years old!

I used to think all my friends had great families when I was growing up. But it wasn't until adulthood that I realized they were really messed up! I've learned that every family is "dysfunctional" to some degree. Yep, some are just more dysfunctional than others.

Now, I am not saying that what happened to you in childhood doesn't matter. I'm not saying you don't have trauma from it or that you should just "get over it".

But you have to come to the realization, at some point, that what happened to you in childhood was out of your control.

You have the power to say, "I don't like what happened. I

was not responsible for it. I will not let those things define who I am."

And you have the power to make the change. But it comes from you.

You may need spiritual support and reliance on the Almighty God to help you to get there, but you've got to be the one to initiate that change.

Stop looking to your parents to heal you. Stop looking to them to tell you what to do.

You might ask for their suggestions or their perspective, but it's up to you. You have to grow up and parent yourself if necessary. You have to cut out those bad roots in order to grow healthy ones.

Good parenting encourages children to become independent adults. If you didn't get that — it doesn't mean you can't develop the skills to take care of yourself in adulthood. Remember what I said about family in Lesson #8. Who are the people who support and encourage you? Tap into the lessons, reminders and positivity they share with you.

If you keep carrying the baggage of a bad childhood, it will weigh you down.

So make this your mantra: "I cannot control what happened to me as a child, but I can control what I do as an adult." I have learned that is how you can own your reality and release yourself from the past.

## LESSON #10

BUY YOUR OWN FLOWERS. THEY'RE NOT GOING TO BE ANY MORE BEAUTIFUL COMING FROM SOMEONE ELSE.

My husband and I celebrated our 38th anniversary on October 8$^{th}$, 2021. And for many, many years before we got married, I told him, "I love flowers! I really, really, love them! HINT HINT!!"

Yet it was only every now and then he would remember to get me flowers. I couldn't even expect them on our anniversary. He's just not that kinda guy.

I used to get angry and say, "Well, the least you could do was get me some flowers!"

Eventually it dawned on me that I was trying to force him to show his love the way I wanted. But that way was just awkward and goofy for him.

The way he shows me love is what he saw his father do for his mother. So my husband gets up on a snowy day and shovels the driveway. Then he turns on my car so it's warm when I get in. That's his way of saying "I love you."

I didn't think of it that way. I wanted flowers because that's how I thought you show love.

## LESSON #10

My husband is a do-er. He's a problem-solver. He's a protector — and that's what I really love about him.

I had to accept that he's not a very good "flower guy" — but that doesn't mean I can't have flowers in my life!

I realized that whether the flowers came from him or from me — they're still beautiful! And I enjoy seeing them in the house.

So about 20 years ago, I joined a 'Flower of the Month' club. Every month I got the most gorgeous bouquet of flowers. And it just made me smile. At first, the bouquets arrived without a note. But then I started adding scheduled messages like:

"Carline, You're awesome!"
"Carline, You ROCK."
"Carline, You Go Gurrlll"

And I really loved reading those little boosts of encouragement that came with those beautiful flowers!

So my lesson learned is this: If you want flowers — get your own!

Don't turn those flowers into drama. Don't convince yourself these flowers would be so much better if they came from your spouse. Don't force your mate to show love YOUR way.

Now — it's important to know what you need and to talk to your partner about those needs.

What I love more than flowers is hugs. I am a big-time hugger. I mean, if I see you, I'm hugging you. I'll hug you even if I don't know you. If we are friends, I will hug you to death.

But again, that's not my husband. I joke that to get a hug from him I have to explain why I need it. And he'll ask, "What's wrong? Are you sick?" OK — so that's a bit of an exaggeration, but not too much!

One year, for an anniversary gift, I told him I wanted him to hold my hand while we walked. He said, "Why? There's no traffic, you're not gonna fall." I was like, "Dangit! I just want you to hold my hand because I like the feeling of you holding my hand!"

So I have to be very specific.

But I will say this: When my husband wants to give you a hug — it's amazing. He goes all in. But he can also go weeks without a hug. I can't.

So I have to let him know when it's hug time!

## LESSON #11

**TELL YOUR MENTORS "THANK YOU". SHOW YOUR APPRECIATION BY DOING SOMETHING VERY NICE FOR THEM.**

About 10 years ago, I decided I was going to spend the year showing appreciation to my mentors — and anyone who made a difference in my life. They could be from my childhood... while raising my kids... or in my career.

I created a list of people who made an impact in my life. Then I scheduled a time to physically visit each and every one of them. It didn't matter if it was just for a few hours or a few days. I was going to visit and spend time with them — and make it a special occasion.

I wanted to thank them face-to-face!

And I said to each of them "Let me tell you how you changed my life." And I did. I wish I had written a book about that year. It was amazing!

Once a month, I went through my list and scheduled a visit. One month I went to see Mrs. Gwendolyn Hall, who taught me how to crochet, play ping-pong and kept me out of trouble when I was growing up.

From the age of 7 through to 14, she kept an eye on me at the Rec Center at Keene Elementary School in Washington

D.C. — Mrs. Hall made me feel loved. She kept me on the right path. And she gave me a safe place to hang out after school.

When I called her, I was living in Georgia and she was in Maryland. So I told her I was flying up to have lunch with her. She could pick any restaurant she wanted. It was my treat. And of all the fancy restaurants in Maryland — she picked Applebee's!

That cracked me up! Maryland is known for its amazing crab cakes — but we went to Applebee's!

During lunch I told her: "I'm going to smother you with love and appreciation. So don't interrupt me!" I shared with her specific examples of how she helped mold my life. How she was an amazing role model. We both just started crying right there in Applebee's. It was beautiful.

Then later in the year I flew out to the West Coast and spent a week visiting my favorite people there.

First stop was to visit my friend Sherrie Burgess Brooks — the only person I still keep in touch with from my California college days. Sherrie was my next-door neighbor in off-campus housing during my freshman year. We quickly became friends.

What I appreciated the most about Sherrie was her willingness to share her family with me. Her parents, Leroy and Rosemary Burgess invited me to their home. I hung out with her brother Fritz. And I'm thankful still to this day that her sister Rhonda gave me legal advice that helped me get out of debt many years later.

Sally Castion became my "spiritual mom" when I moved 3,000 miles away from home to attend the University of Southern California. Whenever I was dealing with a problem, Sally found a way to share a principle from the Scriptures to give me insight and direction.

She never told me what to do. She just shared experiences and gave me guidance. I didn't realize then that Sally was teaching me powerful lessons that I use in copywriting to this day: Show your prospect the benefits and help him come to his own conclusion!

Over 40 years later, I still keep in touch with Sally and her husband George. She was an influencer in my life and I still cherish that day we spent together.

After visiting Sally, I got on a red eye to Las Vegas to see Cynthia Epps, another special "spiritual mom" to me. Cynthia and her husband Kevin picked me up at the airport. I told her we could do whatever she wanted for the day. She said, "Let's just talk for now."

We ended up sitting and talking at her kitchen table — staying up all night. We just laughed, cried, hugged and reminisced about our adventures. And we kept talking until she and Kevin drove me to the airport. It was awesome.

Then in April, I flew to Sarasota, Florida to have lunch with Clayton and Wendy Makepeace. Clayton taught me what I know about copywriting. I owe him a debt of gratitude. Wendy and I worked at Phillips Publishing together in the late 1980s. So both of these folks are very special to me.

It was fun seeing Clayton and Wendy in their element — eating at their favorite hangout and meeting their local friends. Clayton talked about how much he appreciated that afternoon we spent together for years. When Clayton died suddenly in 2020, I felt comforted that he knew how much I love and respect him.

As the year went by, I spent time with my mom Michelle, my grandmother Mama Da, my aunts Yolande, Maude, Jacqueline and Carol and numerous friends and neighbors. I made sure they knew how I felt about them.

I didn't want to get a phone call saying, "Hey, did you hear that So-and-So died?" I didn't want to regret not telling the people who are special to me how much they enriched my life.

So my lesson learned is this: You didn't get to where you are without help, support and mentoring. Take the time and show appreciation while you can. Tell these folks so often that they say, "OK, stop. I get it. You LOVE me!" Whatever it takes, make sure they know. They may be having doubts, tough times or feeling down. Your words may come at the perfect time. And now you can have a powerful impact on *their* life.

## LESSON #12

### DON'T BE STUPID WITH YOUR MONEY. IT CAN GO FASTER THAN IT CAME.

At copywriting and marketing seminars, I talk to many young people in their twenties who made a huge amount of money in a short time. They consistently do the same stupid things.

They go out and buy a sports car because they've always wanted a Ferrari or a Lamborghini. You just spent $250,000 on a car and where are you going? You work from home — and you work all the time! Sure, it looks like you've "made it". And you feel important. But don't be stupid with your money.

You see the cycle repeating — just like young athletes who become overnight sports stars: From poverty to multi-millionaire — and back to poverty again!

They never developed the in-between stage of learning how to handle money.

Then an injury takes them out. Their contract fizzles and the overhead from their luxuriant lifestyle bankrupts them. They have no savings or investments in place to fall back on.

So if you suddenly find yourself making a lot of money, yes — it's OK to do something to celebrate. But don't blow it on material stuff that depreciates!

Take care of the people who took care of you... buy your mother a house... pay off your parent's mortgage... get your siblings cars if they really need them. But you've got to take care of yourself. You must remember the money can go as fast as it comes — if you don't manage it wisely.

Lesson learned: If you don't take care of yourself — you can't take care of anybody else.

And if you *must* have that expensive sports car — then lease it for one year. Trust me: In six months, the novelty will wear off. That car will sit in your garage more than you use it!

You won't take that "baby" out when it's raining. You'll get sick of parking far away so no one scratches it in the parking lots. And the depreciation will kill you! Please, just get a short-term lease on the dang car — until the novelty wears off.

As an entrepreneur or a freelancer, you can have a phenomenal year and the next year can absolutely suck. So you have to live in the middle range. If you have a great year, take that extra bump in income and put it away for that rainy day that will surely come. You are going to have down months when you need to draw from your savings. Make sure that your savings account is padded!

Another lesson learned: Treat money with respect. Use it to take care of your needs — not to show off.

If you don't have a place to live, buy your house. Pay cash for it if you can. Mortgages are overrated. It's a good feeling to have your house paid off.

Pay off your debt. Take care of your family. Invest your money wisely.

The reality is that money is just a vehicle. It is not your happiness. It is not your love. Money itself is not going to keep you warm. It's simply a means to help you achieve those goals.

Keep your priorities straight.

## LESSON #13
### THAT CHECK IS NOT ALL YOURS.

When I started my freelance business, I had a simple plan. When money came in, I divided and saved it in four "buckets". That way I didn't have to think about what to do with the check — it was automatic. Here's what I did:

- Bucket #1: 30% taxes
- Bucket #2: 20% savings
- Bucket #3: 5% charity
- Bucket #4: 45% living expenses

It didn't matter if the check was $100, $1000, $10,000, or $100,000 — I didn't deviate from the formula!

When you're in a 9-to-5 job, "Uncle Sam" gets his tax money before you even see that paycheck. You live on your net income. But when you run your own business, you get gross income. And that can be dangerous if you're not careful! You've got to put money aside for those taxes — or you're going to be in serious trouble come tax time. That's why I take out that 30% immediately and save it for taxes. I overestimate on the 30% because I'd rather have money left over than money due when it's time to pay taxes!

I use the 20% savings to invest in me and my business. I invest that money in mutual funds, money market accounts and so on. That is my "grow" money. This income allows me to fund new ventures and try new ideas for my business.

The 5% charitable donation is my opportunity to give back. It's to remind me of how fortunate I am and how I can help others. This amount eventually grew to 7%. While it took my net income down to 43% — I experienced many joys and blessings from this automatic giving.

Decide how you're going to do something wonderful with your charitable money. You can donate it all to one charity or split it up among different causes you want to support. Whatever you decide — just make sure you do it — and do it regularly.

So from Day One of my freelance career — I trained myself to live off less than 50% of my income. This taught me a valuable lesson: I can live below my means. I don't need to impress anyone with what I have — and I don't need to get myself into debt just because I can generate a large income.

My little "four-bucket" formula is also a protection for me creatively. Because I have savings, I don't have to work with clients I don't like or take on projects that don't interest me just to make money to cover my expenses.

Plus: If I don't get paid on time by clients — my bills still get paid thanks to a padded savings account. And I don't give off that "desperation vibe" because money is tight. Here's what I mean: If you absolutely *have* to have a check to pay your rent or your mortgage — you're going to start sweating bullets when that check is late. Then you'll do dumb things like take on another job for a whole lot less money — just because you need the cash. That can hurt you in the long run. After all — why would that client want to pay you more money in the future? You already discounted your fees!

So make sure you have a financial cushion so you can say NO to projects that don't interest you. If you can cover your bills, you're in a better position to negotiate and even walk away from a project. That's powerful!

## LESSON #14

**WEAR YOUR SPECIAL CLOTHES AND GOOD JEWELRY EVERY DAY — EVEN TO WALMART. BEING ALIVE AND HEALTHY IS ENOUGH OF AN OCCASION.**

When I was a kid my mom had a china cabinet where she kept the "good" china. Every six months or so, it was my job to take the china out, clean it and put it back in the cabinet.

We probably used that china five times in my whole childhood! Those fancy dishes just sat in that dang cabinet gathering dust. Even though my mom loved that "Black Rose" china pattern, we *never* used it. It just sat there!

So when my mom gave me some "good china" for my 8th wedding anniversary — I was NOT keeping it in the china cabinet. We used the "Pink Rose" china every day. When Mom saw I was giving my kids their morning cereal in the good china — she was mortified! She said, "China is for special occasions!" Well in this house Mom, eating cereal is special!

Think about the "good" clothes you only wear on special occasions. How often have you taken them out only to realize you can't fit them anymore — and then had to go and buy *more* "good" clothes that you'll save for a special occasion again?

This is a lesson my cousin Pat Louhisdon taught me.

One day I asked Pat if she wanted to run to Walmart with

me. When I arrived to pick her up, she came out of her house all decked out — looking gorgeous! I, on the other hand, was wearing a stained t-shirt and sweatpants.

I said, "Dang, we're just going to Walmart!" She said, "It doesn't matter. Wherever I go, I'm going to look nice. It makes me feel good." Then she said...

"Wear yo clothes, girl!"

That was a lightbulb moment for me.

I decided to adopt Pat's attitude. Now I use what I have and don't save anything for "special occasions". I got rid of my fancy jewelry I never wore — and I wear the stuff I kept, every day and 'just because'.

I kept my wedding rings, my favorite diamond earrings and a Mother's ring my daughter #1 gave me decades ago. The ring has each of my kids' names and birthstones on it. It's one of my prized possessions. That's it. That's my expensive jewelry collection — and I wear it whether I'm working at home or getting dressed up for a special occasion.

If I can't wear it every day, I don't need it.

Now — I do love funky, costume jewelry and handmade stuff with sentimental value. For example, my grandson Maverick made me a necklace recently from some string and a pretty shell he found at the beach. Well, that's now one of my precious necklaces and I'm going to wear it 'til that string breaks or the shell crumbles.

I don't spend tons of money on clothes. Never have. I shop at Marshalls... TJ Maxx... Ross... Target... Walmart — and of course, Amazon! I buy stuff at a reasonable price and when I get tired of them — I donate them!

Now don't get me wrong — I love clothes — but I love money in the bank more. I would rather fund my savings account than bankroll fashion designers. And I get a thrill when I find a great deal. For my daughter #1's wedding, I found a brand-new designer gown that cost $508 but I paid just $77 for it. And I looked GOOD!

I love that Michelle Obama wears clothes from Target along with her other fancy designers.

So these days, I wear my favorite diamond earrings with my seashell necklace and I put on my TJ Maxx t-shirt and GAP jeans when I go to Walmart.

I look cute and feel good without breaking the bank.

## LESSON #15

A GOOD BRA CAN MAKE YOU LOOK FIVE POUNDS LIGHTER. MY FAVORITE IS THE NATORI YOGI SPORTS BRA.

Any woman who is a D-cup or larger knows my struggle.

I spent *years* trying to find the right bra.

A bra that is comfortable... that you can wear for hours... and gives you the lift and the look that you want. That is harder than finding a "needle in the haystack".

And through the years my boobs — AKA "The Girls" — have changed drastically in size. If I had stopped having children after my daughter #3, I would be a 34C — which in my mind is the perfect size for me. But then I had my son and "The Girls" blew up! The C cup became a D. Then a DD. Then (yikes!) a DDD! And I almost passed out when I once measured an "F" cup!

I looked like the capital letter "P"!

During those stages, it was nearly impossible to find a bra that looked good and fit right.

Then I stumbled on Natori bras — and the heavens opened and said "Behold! Your savior!" I'm not kidding — Natori bras saved me from back aches... sore shoulders... and embarrassing "uni-boobs"! You know what a "uni-boob" is right? It's when you can't tell one boob from the other. "The Girls" get smashed together and look like one huge, round pillow!

I'm telling you right now — I would be a spokesperson for Natori bras in a heartbeat!

After searching for over 15 years — I finally found the Natori sports bra. It was love at first try-on! Absolutely perfect for me in a 34DD. I bought 10 bras every year just for my workouts. Life was good — until Natori stopped making the bra. Without telling me! If I had known I would've bought their ENTIRE inventory.

I can't believe I never wrote down the name and style of that bra. I just assumed it would always be around.

I couldn't find the sports bra anywhere. Not in stores. Not on Amazon. Not even on Ebay. I contacted Natori several times directly and got the same answer. "The bra is discontinued. No further update." Aargh!

I had worn out my bras to where you could see the underwire. The hooks had broken off and I was keeping the bras together with safety pins! I spent a fortune trying to find a suitable replacement. Nothing felt right.

And then — Natori came through for me again! They had a new bra in their collection!

It's called the Natori Yogi Bra.

Oh my goodness! This sports bra is so comfortable — I can sleep in it! This time a 34DDD was the perfect fit. The wide straps don't dig into my shoulders. It gives me a nice smooth look. I can run without getting two black eyes. "The Girls" even look a little smaller. I just love it! I've trashed all my other bras and "The Girls" are in heaven.

Since my discovery I've told just about anybody who will listen about the Yogi bra! I give them as gifts. Every woman in my company owns at least one. And I keep a nice stockpile — just in case Natori tries to cut me off again!

If you're a full-figure lady still trying to find the right bra — I highly recommend you check out the Natori Yogi bra: https://www.natori.com/new/natori-yogi-bra/. Lately I've found them on Ebay too!

I'm not being compensated for promoting Natori bras. This is my personal testimonial. I know the struggle is real and if you agree that this bra is the answer you've been looking for — let me know. Send me an email at carline@carlinecole.com.

Glad I can help my full-figured female family.

## LESSON #16

### YOUR KIDS WON'T REMEMBER BIG FAMILY EVENTS BEFORE AGE 7 — SO SAVE DISNEY WORLD UNTIL IT COUNTS.

When I was growing up, we didn't go on a lot of vacations. We went to the beach one time — I didn't have a swimsuit — so I had to share one with my sister Viv. We took turns going into the water!

We were not the family that went to the beach every summer... or to the mountains... or camping. My sister, brother and I got shipped off to Philadelphia to spend the summers with my grandmother Mama Da and my cousins.

But I wanted to have the kind of family that did great vacations every year.

So when I became an adult, I decided I was going to relive my childhood with my kids! I could control these things now. So I got to take all the vacations and do all the fun stuff I'd wanted to do as a kid.

We did everything —camping, beach trips, Disney World, domestic and international traveling.

When my son was 4 years old, we took a family trip to Maui. It was awesome! I loved it.

But to this day, my son tells people he's never been to Hawaii! He has no memory of it.

Lesson learned: Do not invest money in big family trips until everyone is old enough to remember them!

Save the money — take the kids camping locally and tell them it's the Grand Canyon. Take them to the zoo and tell them that it was a safari in Africa. They'll be excited to see the lions and tigers and giraffes. You only have to pay for a day trip — and you'll be home by the time they get tired and cranky.

Save the big trips for after the age of 7 when they can really appreciate and remember them.

## LESSON #17

### DON'T MAKE YOUR KIDS YOUR ENTIRE LIFE. YOU REALLY DO WANT THEM TO GROW UP AND MOVE OUT.

My mom taught me this lesson.

Remember why you're a parent. You want to raise human beings to become self-sufficient.

When you have a baby — you're in mommy mode. So love it, absorb it, just totally live it. That's where you're at in your life and that's fine.

But once those babies start to grow — you can't have your life revolve exclusively around your children. Yes, they can take up a precious part of your life — but they should not BE your life.

I hear people say, "The children come first." No — they don't. That's a disservice to the children. If they always come first, you're in danger of raising spoiled brats who become annoying adults.

The children are important, but so is your mate... your God... and your sanity. And without self-care — you're going to raise some messed-up kids.

Be careful what you sacrifice for your children.

Let me give you an example. If you have to choose between

paying for your kid's college education or your own retirement, there's no choice: Retirement wins. Financial expert Suze Orman taught me this lesson.

If your kids want to go to college and you can't afford it, then it's up to them to figure out how to make it happen. There are school loans. They can get a job and pay their own way. They can study part-time. They have options. But have you ever heard of a "Retirement Loan?" I sure haven't!

What happens if you give all your money to your kids for college and they drop out? Or they don't do anything with their degree? Or they're asking "You want fries with that?" after they get their Master's degree? Then what?

They can barely take care of themselves and now you can't take care of yourself either.

And don't put the relationship with your mate on hold until after the kids are grown. You may wake up and realize there's no relationship outside of the kids. That's why many marriages end in divorce after the kids move out. Those kids were the glue that kept the 30-year marriage together.

The kids go off on their own and you look at each other like, "I don't even like you, I haven't spoken to you in years!"

I thought about this a lot when I was younger. So when our kids were little, my husband and I went on monthly dates. Just the two of us.

The kids were not allowed to come and we didn't go out with another couple. It was just the two of us. Sometimes we did look at each other with nothing to say. That's when we knew we needed to work harder on our marriage. Realizing this early in the marriage is much easier to handle than dealing with decades of non-communication.

Invest in your marriage.

## LESSON #18

### IF YOU GIVE A FRIEND $20 AND YOU NEVER SEE HIM AGAIN, IT WAS WORTH IT.

Fool me once, shame on you. Fool me twice, shame on me.

If somebody wants to borrow money from you and you can afford it, then sure — loan them the money. If that's the only reason they want you, you'll know soon enough. If you never see them again, it's worth it. Now you know who that person really is.

Or if you see them again and they still don't pay it off, you understand what the relationship is about to them. So you can decide how far you're willing to invest in that friendship.

Sometimes stuff happens. Loans don't get paid back on time as promised. But it's the responsibility of the borrower to update the lender. The lender shouldn't have to chase down the borrower for repayment.

If you haven't paid me back on one loan, don't come back asking for another.

Lesson learned: I'm not a bank. If I was — I would charge you interest.

But I have another powerful lesson tied into this one: Don't loan money to people and expect you're going to get it back.

If you absolutely need to get that money back, *do not* lend the money. You may never see it again and now you're in a financial mess. Don't put yourself in that position. Only loan money you can afford to lose.

It's the same principle with lending items to people. Don't lend stuff to anyone if you absolutely have to get it back in the same condition you loaned it.

If someone asks to borrow your car, expect it may come back with scratches. Hopefully it won't but if you can live with that scratch, then loan the car.

I found adopting that attitude kept me at peace. Most of the time the loan was repaid and the item was returned in good condition. But when that didn't happen — my blood pressure didn't go up. I didn't harbor any resentment towards that person. I just let it go and moved on. I had already prepped myself for the worst-case scenario — so it's all good.

If it can be fixed or replaced, then it's not a problem. Holding a grudge just makes you tired and bitter!

## LESSON #19

### DON'T CONFUSE "PRINCIPLE" WITH "PETTINESS".

"It's the principle of the matter."

This phrase should be a bell going off in your head — and it should make you ask yourself: *"Is it really?"*

Sometimes it might be a principle. But most often it's just pettiness.

So by asking yourself, *"Is it really?"* you can see the clear picture and your true motive.

Let's say I'm working with a client and something comes up that's outside our original agreement. I could charge them extra for each little thing. But if the client's not getting on my nerves and the request isn't crazy — then I'm just going to go ahead and do the work without asking for more money.

In principle, I *should* ask for more money. But if I charge them for every little thing, it starts to feel petty.

Cover tests are a good example. When I turn in a sales promo I agree to provide two cover tests. If I do, then I've upheld my end of the deal. But most of the time I deliver 3... 5... even 10 cover tests! Why?

Because I know that cover tests can make or break my

promo. It's in my best interest to give the client as many cover tests as possible. I actually increase my odds of getting a winner!

I could be petty about it and charge the client for the additional cover tests. But that wasn't our agreement. And it's not in my best interest in the long run. The big picture is that I want my package to succeed!

The client pays me at least $25,000 to write a sales promo. That's a hefty investment. They can decide to just go with the 2 cover tests and see how they perform. But when I give them more cover tests — they test more! And that increases my odds of success! Many times — it's the third or fifth additional cover that gives me the breakthrough winner!

I would've missed out on that success if I had just stuck to the 2-cover test agreement.

So look at the big picture. Keep the endgame in mind. Remember what you want to accomplish in this situation and don't get petty about the little stuff that comes up along the way.

Sure — you might make a little extra money by charging for additional work. But you can miss out on the potential for making REAL money — tens or hundreds of thousands of dollars in royalties down the road!

Pettiness will bite you in the butt.

## LESSON #20
I LIKE ME. IF YOU DON'T — THAT'S OK. YOUR LOSS.

This is just self-preservation.

When I was a teenager, if somebody didn't like me, I honestly couldn't believe it!

And I would make a serious effort to win them over.

Somehow I got it in my head that it was my duty to make people like me. But that's a heavy load and a lot of hard work. Spending energy to get people to like you is a waste of that energy.

Even in my twenties, I still tried hard to be liked. I wanted that validation and I just couldn't stand the idea that someone didn't like me.

But then, in my thirties, I realized: *You know what? I'm OK.*

I like me.

I would hang out with me. I think I'm a fun person with a nice personality. And if somebody doesn't agree — that's OK too. So my thirties gave me freedom to not care. I loved that time in my life... and my forties?

Well, my forties were like my thirties — but with ten extra years of attitude and experience!

In my fifties — I ditched the attitude and just focused on inner peace. "You do you, Boo!" That's your choice. And you live with the consequences.

So as I'm now entering my sixties — I'm definitely feeling more of an "I ain't got time for that!" vibe. Maybe it's because there's less life expectancy ahead? Who knows? We'll see! In any case — I'm loving it!

Lesson learned: Save yourself decades of frustration. Don't waste your energy worrying about what other people think of you. Focus on what YOU think of you. Be a good person, be somebody you like to be around. If you can't stand yourself, people aren't going to stand you either.

There's a lot of freedom in self-acceptance and in realizing you're not going to make everyone your friend. And that's OK.

The people who are attracted to you and like your personality and character — they're awesome! So focus on them. Work on those relationships.

If I like me — and I like you — then that's great. If it's not mutual — that's OK too. We can move on.

## LESSON #21

### HATE THE ACT, NOT THE PERSON.

This is hard. Really hard.

I've seen some horrific things happen to people I love. And this lesson has really tested my core beliefs.

It forced me to really dig into what my spirituality means: *Do you really believe in forgiveness? What does that mean?*

Originally, I thought if I forgave someone it meant I was excusing their behavior. But I couldn't do that, so I really had to figure out how to forgive the person — even if I will never be OK with what they did.

This lesson was really driven home when one of my family members was physically attacked a few years ago. I saw RED.

I was so angry that I wanted to do anything I could to get back at that person. It was like a fire, totally consuming. Eventually I realized I couldn't move on with my life if I was carrying this rage inside of me.

I had to learn to accept that the act was despicable. But I couldn't stop there. I had to forgive the person who did it — whether or not they asked for the forgiveness. The forgiveness is for my healing. Not anyone else's. Forgiveness allows me to move on with my life — and not to get frozen in time.

Dang! That's REALLY hard.

People make mistakes. I make mistakes! And I would hate it if somebody kept bringing up a mistake I made years ago, especially if I had tried to make it right. I would want them to help me move on.

Now, I'm not going to be best friends with the person that attacked my family member. I'm not going to hang out with them. But I had to separate the human being from the action.

This, honestly, is still a work in progress.

But forgiveness is a release valve that allows you to continue to function.

Forgiveness allows you to acknowledge what happened. And then lets you decide whether you're going to let that moment define the rest of your life.

Forgiveness allows you to go beyond that moment instead of getting stuck at that point in time.

## LESSON #22

**THE DAY YOU GIVE BIRTH, OPEN A "THERAPY FUND". YOUR KIDS CAN USE IT TO FIX ALL THE STUFF YOU SCREW UP WHILE YOU RAISE THEM.**

I should've put more money in that "Therapy Fund".

Now, I think I'm a great mom. I really, really, really do think that. But I also know I probably did stuff that screwed up my kids.

No matter how great a family life you have, something is going to be jacked up.

And everybody is going to experience things from a different perspective. I listen to my kids talk to their friends about their childhood and I have to stop myself from blurting out, "That's not what happened!"

But I'm looking at it from my perspective, not theirs.

To me, my kids had a great life! They had both parents, who loved each other and stayed together. They were never homeless or hungry. They were protected and never experienced serious physical or emotional danger. They had a great support system from friends, family and from our congregation. And — I hugged and kissed them to death.

In my opinion, their childhood would make a boring Lifetime movie! And my husband and I are very proud of that.

Yet they say they experienced "drama".

As they grew up, we started to hear how hard they tried to please us. How much they hated our family routines. How we got on their nerves. What?

At first, I was highly offended. And then I realized, "You know what? No matter how hard we try as parents, we're imperfect. We're gonna screw up."

I'm just glad we screwed up a whole lot less than other parents. I'm glad my kids complained of having to come home at a reasonable time... being forced to eat healthy foods... and having strict parents who really cared about them. I'll take those "faults" any day, any time.

So my lesson to pass on is this: Open up a therapy fund with the birth of your first child. That way the money is there to help your kids if you did or didn't do something in their childhood. If you really messed them up — maybe a therapist can help fix 'em. I am an advocate for getting professional help.

Now, the "therapy fund" became available to my 4 children when they turned 18. They are all in their thirties now. The fund is still available if needed.

## LESSON #23

**THERE'S ALWAYS 10 THINGS YOU'LL HATE ABOUT YOUR MATE. IF YOU SWAP FOR ANOTHER MATE, THAT ONE WILL HAVE 10 THINGS YOU'LL HATE TOO. MIGHT AS WELL STICK WITH WHAT YOU KNOW.**

What I'm talking about is the commitment factor that comes with marriage.

Believe me — when you marry someone, you're going to find at least 10 things that you hate about that person. And whatever those things are — they seldom change.

If you focus on those negatives and let your frustration fester — you're going to get to a point where you can't deal with it anymore.

So you go find another mate. And guess what? That new partner also has 10 things that you're not gonna like either!

At least you know what you are dealing with in the first relationship!

So I try to work with what I've got. It does not serve me to wonder, "Is there someone better out there for me?"

Now, I'm not talking about remaining in an abusive relationship. And I am in no way qualified to tell you whether to stay in your marriage or not.

But what I am certain of is this: If you're fed up with your mate's annoying habits, just remember that you're going to have to deal with annoying habits of another mate!

Be willing to compromise... be willing to let things go... and be willing to speak up.

Sometimes your partner may not know that something makes you mad. If you speak up, you may hear, "Oh, I didn't realize that bothered you. I can stop that, no problem." Or you may hear, "Sorry, I'm not going to change that, you're gonna have to deal with it." Either way — at least you know what's up.

When you harp on things you can't stand about your marriage, it's usually an indication that communication has broken down in the relationship. And when that's the case, every little molehill becomes a mountain.

This is the time to remind yourself that you didn't marry a perfect person and neither did your mate. By the way — you've got at least 10 annoying flaws too!

Focus on the 10 great assets your mate possesses. Write them down and read them often.

Most likely, you got together because you complement each other. Your mate's weakness might be your strength, and vice versa.

Don't use your strength to highlight your mate's weakness. Use that strength to compensate for it so that as a team, you do better together.

## LESSON #24

### THE ONLY PERSON YOU CAN CHANGE IS YOU. AND EVEN THAT'S HARD.

You are the only person you can control.

If you try to control other people, if you try to change other people, it is a waste of time and energy. You cannot change anyone.

If you're a parent, you can try to force your children to some degree. If you're a spouse, you can nag or yell to try to get your mate to see things your way. But the change will not come from you.

Change comes from within. Change comes from the person wanting or needing to make that change personally.

Besides — you need a lot of work done on yourself. Focus on the changes you need to make. That's what is within your control — and it's doable.

For example, if your spouse has an irritating habit, ask yourself "Is it *really* that bad? How can you address the issue? How can you react differently? How can you look at it in a positive light?" These are things that are within your power to change.

If you can discuss it, you may find your mate may be willing to make the change. But if you lecture or demand a "cease and desist" — it's just going to get worse. Your mate will get defensive and shut you out.

Here's something else to keep in mind: You may be the cause of that irritating behavior. It may be your mate's way of dealing with your junk.

If you can acknowledge that imperfection is present in the relationship — then you can look for ways to make an excuse and not accuse.

So ask yourself if you can let it go. If you can, do it.

Not everything needs to be a confrontation.

## LESSON #25

### EXERCISE IS THERAPY. RUNNING KEEPS ME FROM GOING INSANE.

This clicked for me on July 31, 1996, just a few days after I turned 35.

Up until that point, my kids had been my exercise. With 4 very high-energy kids, I was active. I was moving and grooving! I was nursing... feeding... potty-training... picking kids up... and running after them. There was no need for me to "exercise"!

My life was exercise, and boy, did I have nice arms. I didn't lift weights —just kids!

But once they were all in school, I realized I wasn't getting any exercise at all.

I sat in my car for a three-hour round-trip commute to my job. Then I would sit in my chair in the office for eight hours or more. Then when I got home, I was too tired to do anything active!

All the exercise had gone out of my routine. And I could tell it was affecting me in a negative way. My brain didn't feel right. My body started to ache in all kinds of places. My stress level was high. And my nerves were short.

## LESSON #25

I didn't put two and two together until I got up early one day and decided to go for a walk before work.

I only meant to walk around the block, but the air felt so good going inside my brain that I ended up walking for an hour! I felt energized when I got home. I was thinking clearer when at work. So the next day I did it again. And the day after that. And I kept on doing it because I liked how I felt after my walks.

But then one day, I was running late — so instead of a morning walk — I decided to run so I could make up for the time.

And that changed everything.

I felt so GOOD! Even better than when I walked. I never considered myself a runner. But when I ran — all my problems seemed minimal. I felt focused. My brain kicked into a higher gear. The clarity was addictive!

So even though I was sweaty and my body would hurt — it was a good kind of hurt.

One time it rained for a few days in a row so I couldn't get out to run. And I could *immediately* tell the difference. People annoyed me quicker. My thoughts wouldn't come together clearly. My stress level rose. And I was just mean. That's when it dawned on me: Exercise is my therapy.

And exercise continued to be my therapy all through my forties, fifties and now into my sixties.

In fact, when I was 59, I was running five miles a day, six days a week. Then one day my daughter #1 called me and told me she was training for a half-marathon —which is 13.2 miles. I thought she was crazy. But it made me wonder, "Why not try it?

So that morning instead of 5 miles — I ran 7!

The next day — I ran 8 miles. A few days later — I ran 10 miles!

By now — I had the confidence to try the half-marathon! However — when I got to 11 miles — I hit the proverbial "wall". I thought I was going to DIE.

When I told my daughter, she said, "Mom! You've gotta train properly and eat snacks along the way. You just ran 11 miles without any fuel. No wonder you feel bad!"

OK — so I tried again. I packed a banana with peanut butter along with my water. At 10 miles, I ate my snack and I definitely felt a surge of energy. I not only made it to 13.2 — I showed off and ran 13.5 miles!

And a few weeks later — I ran another half-marathon!

Want to know the cool thing about this experience?

I documented it on my Carline Cole YouTube video channel! So if you want to experience this journey with me — you can watch the playlist at: https://www.youtube.com/c/CarlineCole

Like I said — I feel good! And now I know at 60 years old — I can run a half-marathon! I couldn't have done that in my twenties. I had knee pain in those days. But today, my knees feel great. Being an alternative health copywriter has its perks. I've learned to take nutritional supplements to regenerate cartilage between my joints and strengthen my bones.

So for me, exercise is not an option. It's a way of life if I want to stay sane... feel a sense of control when life goes haywire... and think clearly.

Exercise is my drug of choice — and yes, I'm hooked!

## LESSON #26

DON'T SIGN NON-COMPETE AGREEMENTS. THEY PROTECT THE BUSINESS BUT KEEP YOU IN CHAINS.

I have never signed a non-compete agreement and I never will.

That's because I have never been presented with a non-compete agreement that's beneficial for the employee or contractor. However, they are highly beneficial for the company.

To me, non-competes are just a way for a company to put you in golden handcuffs after they've benefited from your hard work and you part ways!

Non-competes make me really mad. You work your butt off to become an expert in your craft. And that's why the company hired you in the first place. And now — when the relationship is over — you're prevented from making an income in your area of expertise. You've got to sit on the sidelines for years and let your talent go to waste.

You can't work for the company's competitors. You can't start a business that's "competitive" with theirs. So your hands are tied and you can't provide for your family.

Oh, heck no!

You may get an incentive for signing a non-compete agreement, like stock options, a fancy title, etc... But you are still ultimately cutting off your ability to capitalize on your talents when the work relationship ends.

And believe me — that relationship can end much sooner than anticipated — i.e. you get fired!

The trade-off between loyalty to a company and inability to control my destiny was always too much for me to bear.

I may rethink this view if I get offered $100 million not to work. But my non-competes never came near that amount.

I have seen former co-workers who were unceremoniously terminated suffer financially because of their non-competes. I have seen others go "under the radar" and break their non-competes in order to provide for their families.

But if I sign an agreement, I honor it. That's why I don't sign non-competes.

When I worked at Phillips Publishing as a Marketing Director, I was told that I couldn't advance in my career without signing a non-compete. If I aspired to become a Group Publisher or Vice-President, the non-compete was non-negotiable.

So I never became a Vice-President at Phillips. Instead, I became President of Cole Marketing Solutions, Inc — my freelance copywriting business that I could start without any golden handcuffs — the day after I left Phillips.

I think "Madam President" suits me much better anyway.

## LESSON #27

### BLACK PEOPLE DO GO TO THERAPISTS — BUT THEY'RE CALLED "GIRLFRIENDS".

There's a stigma in the African-American culture about seeing a therapist. OK — to put it point blank — many family members tell me: Therapists are for white people. Or as my neighbor once said, "Black people don't go to therapy, we go to church!"

The truth is therapy can benefit anyone who needs it. And there's a lot of black people I know who need therapy!

But sometimes, going to therapy isn't an option. That's why we have friends. For me, prayer, exercise and my girlfriends help keep my head on straight.

My girlfriends really are my therapists. They help me see a situation from a different perspective. A therapist tries to guide you and direct you to be your better self — and helps you overcome obstacles you struggle to deal with.

My girlfriends have been doing that for me all my life!

I have a core group I trust. I can talk to them about whatever is on my mind. They know me well enough to tell me the truth — and they don't care if I get mad at them or not!

None of them are "yes people". I need my inner circle to keep it real — so I can stay grounded.

I love my girlfriends so much because they're not afraid to tell me what I need to hear. And I respect them enough to believe what they're saying is coming from a place of goodness and honesty.

There's no animosity. No hidden agenda. I might not agree with what they say but I respect their right to say it.

Now, they're not "one size fits all" therapists. I go to specific girlfriends about issues I know they can help me with. I tap into their individual strengths. For example...

... I talk about marriage stuff with my married girlfriends. It's not that my single friends don't have insights that can be beneficial — I just want someone who's in the trenches with me.

If I need to talk about my children, I've got girlfriends raising children or with grown children. If it's business stuff, I'm talking to the ones who own businesses. I want guidance and direction based on the knowledge and experience each person can contribute. So I treat them as board members of the Carline Anglade-Cole company (see lesson #58).

My girlfriends know I do this and many of them do the same with me. They know not to come to me if they don't want to hear the raw truth.

We give each other free therapy sessions!

They know me. They really, really know me. No matter what kind of success I may have, they knew me back in the day — where I started and how I struggled. I've been told a few times, "Don't be getting all uppity with me! We shared underwear back when we were broke, so I don't want to hear it!"

I love these women. They're every shade of the rainbow and represent many decades in the aging process.

I like to tap into the knowledge of those who are much older and wiser than I am. They're my window into the future.

Whenever I hit a new milestone in my age, whether it was turning 40, 50, and now 60, I ask: "What am I in for? Tell me the best thing about being 60. Tell me the worst thing for you about being 60." Putting out some feelers to figure out what's in store has been great. It helps keep me sane and grounded.

It also keeps me close to people who have invested in me. They're invested in my happiness... my health... my career... and my family. They are just a few in number and they know who they are. And they know I love them to the moon and back.

While this black woman doesn't have a professional therapist — I definitely go to therapy every single day — thanks to my home girls.

## LESSON #28

### WHEN I LOOK FAT, I SLAP THE HECK OUT OF THE MIRROR AND THEN WADDLE AWAY!

You know those days when you get out of bed, you're feeling good, you're feeling energetic, and then you look in the mirror — and there's a roll of fat staring back at you?

UGH. It can wreck your whole day!

Or maybe you have a bad hair day, or there's something weird going on with your skin.

That stuff used to throw me off my A-Game.

When I was younger, I used to wear my hair straight, even though I have naturally curly hair. I spent hours getting rid of every bend or wave even in my scalp. And then humidity hit! My hair would explode and turn into a giant poof ball. And when I looked in the mirror — I just wanted to cry.

For so many years, I allowed the mirror to determine what kind of day I was going to have. Seeing that belly poking out or my boobs looking gi-normous would just mess up my day.

I had to learn to stop giving the mirror all that power. So I decided I'm not doing self-hate anymore. Mirror —you better be a friend, or you can get the heck out of my face!

My cousin Sandy Ferguson has the right attitude. She says,

## LESSON #28

"When I look in the mirror, I see what I see. When I walk away — it's everybody else's problem!"

Look — none of us are perfect, yet we are our own biggest critics. I will look at a picture and think, "Oh man, my arms look flabby! And where did those wrinkles come from? or "Yikes! Is that a double chin?" Then literally a few minutes later, somebody else will look at the same picture and say, "Wow, your arms look great! You look so young and thin!"

It's all a matter of perspective. We are so hard on ourselves — yet most of the time people don't even notice what we get fixated and upset about!

I got to a point where I realized I just had to do my best. Sure, I don't weigh what I did at 30, but I'm healthy and I'm happy. I'm exercising a whole lot more. I sleep great. So why do I care about what I weighed at 30?

I remember reading about an experience of the actress Kirsty Alley when she talked about her weight in an interview. She said she looks back at herself when she was in her twenties or thirties, when she weighed 140 pounds and thought she was too fat. But now that she's older, she realizes she was skin and bones back then and just didn't see it.

It's ridiculous what we go through because we just can't see ourselves the way we are. We focus too much on perceived flaws.

So if you want to enjoy an additional three or four years of your life — then stop worrying about what you see in the mirror.

I'm not saying to just let go of caring about your health. But just do what you can. If you're trying to stay within your weight range, exercise and eat well most of the time — and you still don't like what you see in the mirror — ask yourself:

"Why not? Why don't I like this person in that reflection?

Is the extra 5 or 10 pounds making me a bad person?" I don't think so. And neither do you.

Look at your life... are you healthy? Do you have good relationships? Do you have a strong support system? Do you like your job? Are you doing things to help others?

Those are the things you want to measure to determine your true happiness, not the scale — and definitely not the mirror.

## LESSON #29

### IF YOU WANT TO BE A WRITER, WELL DANG IT, YOU GOTTA WRITE!

When I give a seminar or I'm teaching a group of aspiring copywriters — one of the first questions I ask is: "How many of you want to be successful writers?"

Everybody's hands go up.

Then I ask, "How many of you write 3 times a week?"

Most of the hands go down.

"Twice a week?"

Even more hands go down.

"Every day?"

Barely a hand to be seen!

This might seem like another "DUH" moment — but if you want to be a good writer — you've got to WRITE regularly!

I'm not saying you have to be on the computer every day writing for a project. But you've got to write. And there are many opportunities for you to write.

Write a testimonial about a good experience you had with a product.

Write a complaint letter about a bad experience you had with a business.

Write a letter to a friend.

Keep a journal.

And if you don't know what to write about — well write about that!

These are easy ways to practice your writing skills. It doesn't have to be the Great American Novel or the bestselling promotion copy of all time. You just need to get in the habit of writing, telling stories and having conversations in print.

And if you specifically want to be a sales writer — then practice that skill throughout the day. For example...

Write a letter to a friend who owes you money. How do you convince that friend to pay up? Do you use the direct approach or a story approach or do you appeal to emotions like guilt...anger...or sadness?

How would you convince another friend to go rock climbing for the first time? What proof elements would you use to ensure safety? Why should your friend trust you? What obstacles do you need to overcome?

This is all copywriting!

So even if you don't have a client — you can still sharpen your copywriting skills with the people in your life.

Years ago, for career day — I spoke at my daughter's fifth-grade class. I had to explain to them what a copywriter does. So I said:

"How many of you have written a letter to your parents or a family member to ask them to buy you a present or help you with a problem?"

Lots of hands went up.

I said, "Congratulations! You just wrote a sales letter."

Then I asked "How many of you got what you asked for?"

A few hands went up.

Then I said "Woo hoo! You just got a killer control!"

Writing is a muscle that gets stronger with use.

I look at past promotions I've written and I CRINGE! The copy was terrible! I'm a much better writer now. But guess what? The copy did its job. It worked at the time. It became a control.

And yes — I am a better writer now!

## LESSON #30
### BE AFRAID — AND DO IT ANYWAY!

This is my mantra for copywriting. This is my mantra for business. This is my mantra for LIFE. This lesson opened up amazing opportunities and unforgettable experiences for me.

It's now gotten to the point that if I don't experience a little fear about a new venture — I'm not going to do it.

I'm not talking about taking ridiculous risks with your life. This is not about thrill-chasing. I'm talking about calculated risks that get you outside of your comfort zone.

For me — the feeling of trying new ventures and ideas is like being on a rollercoaster. The tension builds up and up and up — and then when that drop suddenly happens — you just gotta hold on and enjoy the ride!

So in copywriting... in business... and in life — I look for opportunities to take me out of my comfort zone — and discover the unknown. And it's been a heck of a ride! For example:

**In copywriting:** For years a German health company tried to get me to work with them. I just wasn't sure this was something I wanted to do or could do well. Then in 2019 — I decided to go for it. But I was going to do it my way.

The client initially wanted me to write the copy in English and they would have it translated. But I know my style of writing and word choices can be difficult to translate. I mean, I use a lot of slang and colloquialism. When I saw a sample of their translated copy — I cringed. They had sucked the life out of my words.

So I agreed to work with them but on my terms: I would translate the copy in German and send them the final. By the way — I may be half-German — but I speak no German. Zilch. But I have a friend named Maria Charagh who is fluent in German and English. So I worked closely with Maria to translate the copy MY way. I turned her into the "German Carline". The results?

The first promotion "Wenn der Blutfluss Kaputt Geht" (translated: When Blood Flow Goes Bad) KICKED BUTT! The client hadn't seen results like that from any other copywriter. Was this a fluke?

Well — the second... third... and the fourth promotions also became killer controls! So being afraid and doing it anyway turned me into a successful international copywriter!

**In business**: My husband and I moved to the Atlanta area right when the housing market crashed. In 2007 you could buy a 3-bedroom, 2-bath ranch home for less than a luxury car. Our plan was to buy one or two homes and turn them into rental properties.

I had little experience in real estate and property management — so it was kinda scary. But I saw an opportunity and convinced my husband to go for it! So we started Carmick Properties.

The USP (unique selling proposition) of the company was simple: "Our house... is YOUR home." And customer service was paramount. We guaranteed phone calls would be answered and repairs made in a timely manner.

We purchased foreclosures, gave them luxury upgrades and kept the rent reasonable. We grew Carmick Properties from 2 rentals to 25. And we maintained a 97% rental occupancy during the 14 years we ran the company. We even had a waiting list for folks who wanted to rent our properties!

When the market rebounded and my husband wanted to retire from the property management business — we sold the homes and cashed out. Being afraid and doing it anyway turned us into real estate tycoons.

**In life**: I fell in love with Mickey Cole when I was 17 years old. There was just something special about this guy. He could always make me laugh — even in the worst of times. So I took a chance and said "I do". Scary? You bet!

We were 22 years old and so broke we couldn't even pay attention! But man oh man has it been an amazing roller coaster ride with this guy. After 38 years of marriage — I'm still looking forward to the next thrill! Being afraid and doing it anyway gave me the love of my life.

Take a chance. It's OK to be afraid.

## LESSON #31

IT'S GOOD TO HAVE A MORAL COMPASS. MINE IS THE BIBLE.

Your compass is only as good as the direction it gives you. If north is in the right place, you're good to go. But if your compass is off, even by a little bit, you're going to end up lost.

When I became one of Jehovah's Witnesses over 40 years ago, I made the Bible my moral compass. It is the foundation of my life and my belief system is based on what the Bible says. When I'm not sure about something, I go back to my moral compass to look for guidance, stories and examples that can help me make my decision.

And I have always been able to find one! It is amazing — it doesn't matter if it's about choosing a mate... friendship... business... or whatever! There is a guiding principle in the Bible I can find to make a good decision. For example...

Let's say I'm dealing with a client and they've wronged me in some way. Maybe it's escalated to the point of pursuing legal steps. Well, I go back to my moral compass: If my foundational belief is that I treat people with kindness and respect, then that should guide my decision.

Even if I know that I'm right and the client is at fault, I can decide — "OK, can I let myself be wronged? Is it going to kill me? Do I share some responsibility in this situation too? Am I being principled or petty?" (Lesson #19.)

If I'm trying to be a follower of Jesus Christ, what would He do in this situation?

Well, He would seek peace. So how do I go back to the client to work it out? What can we do to turn this into a win-win situation?

The solution may not be perfect, but I will try to seek peace and get the situation taken care of. I don't do the litigation stuff. I hate the idea of both of us giving money to attorneys — so they get rich and we're still not happy!

I want to make decisions that make me feel good about myself and that feel true to my belief system. At my core, I love people. I don't have to agree with their decisions and choices. But I respect their rights to make them and I expect them to respect mine.

Even if you don't practice a faith — you need guidance and direction in your life. Some people choose politics or science as their moral compass. Not judging — just advising you to make sure you choose a moral compass that's not fundamentally broken.

## LESSON #32

### GETTING LOST IS HOW I DISCOVER NEW PLACES AND NEW FRIENDS. UNFORTUNATELY, I CAN'T FIND THEM AGAIN.

Don't give me directions by using words like "Go north." I am directionally challenged and my brain just shuts down when I hear words like that.

Tell me to take my next right, drive straight for a few minutes and if I see the big oak tree on the left, I've gone too far.

I can handle those kinds of directions. I do not know which way north is (I may have a moral compass like I mentioned in Lesson #31 but I don't use a real compass!).

I've accepted that I am directionally challenged. And I've learned to compensate for it.

So I make getting lost part of my plan. It's going to happen, even when I have directions! I don't do it intentionally — it just happens. Fortunately for me, I love people. I will talk to ANYONE, ANY TIME!

I have *no* problem pulling up at a gas station to ask for directions or hollering at someone on a street corner to come help me.

And I have stumbled into the most amazing experiences that would never have happened to me if I hadn't gotten lost.

Getting lost has taught me there may be a better or more exciting option.

It's OK to have some adventure and some excitement in your life, because that's when the surprises show up. That's how you grow and learn stuff about yourself. It's how you get to connect with other people and discover new opportunities.

This applies in every part of my life.

When we go on trips overseas, we plan a rough guideline of what we want to do in each place, but we don't do itineraries that have us scheduled to the hour — I hate that! I want to be able to linger... wander off... get lost... figure out how to get back... and do the things the locals are doing.

Having a plan is great, but when serendipity and opportunity show up — invite them into your life!

I try to have a general idea of what I want and where I'm going — but I don't obsessively plan out every detail. That leaves no room for spontaneity.

So getting lost has turned into a way for me to find myself.

## LESSON #33

### END AN EMAIL, LETTER OR NOTE WITH "I LOVE YOU" OR OTHER KIND WORDS.

My mentor, the legendary master copywriter Clayton Makepeace, taught me this lesson.

I always knew how Clayton felt about me — even when he was tearing my copy to shreds. He passed away on March 24, 2020 and I miss him.

The lesson here is simple: Say kind words to the people you care about — because it may be the last time you speak to them.

I still have the last email Clayton sent me — and true to form, he was rippin' into my copy! But at the end, he signed off like he always did: "I love ya!"

Shortly afterwards, he got sick and things snowballed very quickly. Then he was gone. I have kept that email as a reminder of this lesson.

So say what you have to say to people.

Whether it's in copywriting and you're giving crits...

... in business — where you have to deal with lots of personalities and priorities...

... or in your personal life — when you need to have those difficult conversations... .

Don't be afraid to speak your mind. But end it on a positive note.

Let the other person know you're only saying this because you love them and care about them. Let them know that if you didn't care — then you'd just mind your own business and let 'em go ahead and screw up.

Now, maybe you won't always feel that it's appropriate to say "I love you," but there are many simple things you can say to make the point. *You've got this, I miss you, I'm cheering for you, "you're da bomb"* — whatever else you can think of that's positive.

I was sad that Clayton didn't get the chance to write the foreword to my first book, *My Life as a 50+ Year-Old White Male: How a Mixed-Race Woman Stumbled Into Direct-Response Copywriting and Succeeded!* He promised me he would. But I took too long to write the book. I was sad about that, but I didn't have any regrets. Clayton Makepeace knew he was my amazing mentor and a cherished friend who I loved and respected.

And Clayton taught me to make sure the last thing I say to someone is not harsh or mean. That way I don't live with regrets in case those were my last words.

## LESSON #34
### YOUR COPY SUCKS — YOU DON'T!

Before I start the copy critique process with my "C.R.A.Z.Y Copy System Live Mentoring Show" tribe (https://members.carlinecole.com/ready-to-join) — I make them repeat this mantra:

"You're wonderful. You're awesome. Your copy sucks — you don't!"

I do this to take the emotions out of my copy crits. Writers identify with their words. So if someone is attacking your words — it's easy to assume they're attacking you too.

Nothing can be further from the truth. At least when I give copy crits.

As a mentor, copy chief or fellow copywriter — I give crits to help make your copy stronger.

Period.

My crits are never an attack on you personally. But I will admit that my crits can be brutal.

What can I say — the legendary Clayton Makepeace was my copy chief! Blame it on his in-your-face crits! Because the truth is...

... you really need to THANK anybody who's completely honest and frank about your copy. Your writing skills will improve if you just learn to take the punches. I know it did for me!

One time Clayton gave me a crit that said — and I'm making his comment PG-rated...

"You write like a F*%@ing GIRL!"

So I replied...

"I AM a girl!"

But here's the problem...

... I was writing for a male potency product — but my copy wasn't talking to guys! That was a big mistake on my part — and I'm so thankful Clayton brought it to my attention. His crit gave me my very first winner.

And through the years — I will say this — every time Clayton made me cry with his crits — my income skyrocketed!

As I've matured as a copywriter — I developed a great ability to zone in on copy. Nothing else matters. I'm looking for holes to fill and weaknesses to strengthen. So quite often you can hear me say, "Well, this sucks! You blew it here. This is lame. Go back and fix this mess. And what the heck are you talking about?" Again — this is about the copy — not you personally.

Many times, I tear the copy to shreds. That's my job. At this stage — I ain't yo momma. I'm not even your friend. But when the writer makes the fixes and corrects the mistakes — the copy is much stronger and they get good results when it's tested.

And that's when I hear the accolades: "Thanks for beating my copy up Carline, you helped give me a winner! "

I've also learned that "Your copy sucks — you don't!" is a metaphor for life too.

Don't take things personally. If your kid screws up — it

doesn't mean you're a bad parent. If an idea doesn't work — you're not stupid. Or if someone snaps at you because they're having a bad day — shake it off and let it go. It's their problem — not yours.

On the other hand — if a friend is willing to tell you something about yourself that you may not want to hear — my suggestion is to shut your piehole and listen! Sorry — was that harsh? Don't take it that way! Listen to the message. You've got two ears and one mouth for a reason. Listen twice as much as you talk.

Thank the people who stick their necks out to give you advice and direction. You can choose to act on it or not. That's within your power. But thank them. And don't be sarcastic about it. Sincerely thank them, because they care about you.

Don't shoot the messenger.

## LESSON #35
### PROTECT YOUR "ME" TIME. IF YOUR PITCHER IS EMPTY, YOU CAN'T FILL YOUR CUPS.

About 30 years ago I listened to a Nightingale-Conant self-improvement program (on cassette tape!) called *Light His Fire, Light Her Fire*. It was about how marriage mates can bring out the best in each other.

There was one example of the "water pitcher" that stood out. It was a powerful lesson for me.

Imagine you're a large, clear glass pitcher full of red punch. Surrounding you are lots of empty little glasses that represent people and responsibilities in your life.

For me, my glasses were my husband... my four kids... my mom... my job... my friends... my congregation responsibilities... my spirituality... and my neighbors.

So now the speaker says, "Start pouring. Put some punch in all your glasses. Some can get more than others and that's OK. When you pour and pour and pour, what happens? Eventually, the pitcher's empty. You have nothing left to give."

As women — we are notorious givers. We will drain ourselves DRY! But that's self-destructive. Why?

Because your glasses are now going to be thirsty and suffering because you are empty and have nothing to give them.

I was draining myself and not allowing time to refill.

I had to figure out what would fill my pitcher. Back then I loved to sew. I made clothes for me and my kids. Sewing was therapy for me. So I would tell my husband, "I just need an evening to sew without interruption. I just want to be left alone with my sewing machine."

So he would take the kids and I would go off to my little sewing area. I could stay up all night, totally in the zone. I was creating my masterpiece and I felt energized.

Then the next day when the kids got up, I was excited to see them! I wanted to hang out and do stuff with them because now I had the energy. My pitcher was full!

So the lesson learned is: You can't fill your glasses with an empty pitcher. It's the same concept as when you hear the flight attendant say, "Put your mask on first before helping others." You've got to put yourself first so you can take care of the people around you. So what can help you do this?

Is it getting your nails done or a spa day? Is it reading a good book on a lazy weekend? Is it prayer and meditation? Is it going on a trip somewhere new and exciting?

Every time you do something you enjoy, just for yourself — you fill your pitcher. When you keep your own pitcher full, you have the energy and ability to support and nourish the little glasses in your life.

This is not selfishness. It's self-preservation.

## LESSON #36

### PRAY. AND WHEN YOU'RE DONE, PRAY AGAIN. PRAISE JAH!

Prayer has been described many ways, but to me, prayer is a conversation. It's a direct line of communication with the Almighty God. And it's something that I had to learn not to take for granted.

Let's say I wanted to go and talk to the President of the United States right now. There's no way it's going to happen! I can't just pick up the phone and say, "Hey, whatcha doing?"

If I wanted to talk to anyone with any kind of status or fame, I couldn't do it. And yet I have direct access to the Almighty God and I know He listens to me because I've seen my prayers answered.

I have to be careful not to let my busy life affect the quality of my prayers. I'm a chronic multi-tasker and new ideas pop up in my brain all the time. But I've had to learn that prayer is the time to slow down and reflect. I can't squeeze prayer in between writing copy or taking care of my family. I have to respect the privilege of prayer. So how am I still learning to do this?

I have to prioritize prayer like I do other important things in my life. I've learned I can't have a heartfelt prayer at night because I fall asleep. But I am a morning person and that's my peak performance time. So I give prayer that prime time.

My best prayers happen before I get out of bed in the morning. It's a quiet time and I can linger in conversation with my Creator. I can share freely what I feel, need and worry about. I ask for guidance, forgiveness and direction to help me make today the best I possibly can.

So before I even start my day — I've taken care of THE most important thing.

This doesn't mean that's the only time I pray. Throughout the day, I say several prayers. But those are usually short ones to help me cope with immediate issues.

So what do I pray for specifically? I'm not asking for wealth. I'm not praying for someone to be punished because they wronged me. Those aren't the kind of prayers that get answered.

The Bible taught me to seek God's Kingdom first. So I pray about that promised government that is the real solution for mankind's problems. Then I pray for my daily sustenance, to make good decisions, and to help me show love towards other people. I pray for the ability to see the difference between being stupid and smart and to see the difference between principle and pettiness (Lesson #19 again).

I pray for my worldwide brotherhood of nearly 9 million spiritual brothers and sisters. I pray for others — especially my loved ones. And if I know someone's going through a tough time, I include them specifically in my prayers and ask for direction on how I can personally help them.

But prayer is not always about asking. Giving thanks is also a powerful avenue of prayer. So stop and think about what you are thankful for. Did you wake up this morning? Guess what? Many folks didn't. Do you have food in your fridge? Then you're not among those who are starving in the world. Are you relatively healthy? Your legs may be sore — but you've probably got 2 of them! So be thankful for what you have because it could be a lot worse.

The Bible says to "Praise Jah". Well, 'Jah' is just a shortened form of Jehovah. When you say "Hallelujah", you're saying "Praise Jehovah!"

So I praise Jah. I go to Him and I am very confident that my prayers are heard. They may not be answered the way I want but they will be answered in the way I need.

## LESSON #37

GIVE FREELY. GIVE IN SECRET. GIVE INTENTIONALLY. JUST GIVE!

Give every day. Make it part of who you are. Ask yourself what you can give — and remember that it doesn't always have to be money!

You can give your time... experience... and gifts — just to name a few.

If you want a rich and rewarding life — give!

If you know someone is in need, don't wait for them to ask you for help —take the initiative and just do it.

I've learned the expression "If you need anything, just let me know!" may be sincere but it's seldom acted on. It's pretty much the equivalent of saying, "Have a nice day."

Most people won't ask you for help — even if they really need it. But if YOU see where you can assist — then make it easy on them and do what you can.

For example, my husband recently experienced a serious illness. We got lots of phone calls from friends who said "If you need anything, please let me know."

Well, the reality is that we didn't "need" anything.

We have food. My kids were available to help out. There

was nothing that we "needed'. So I said thank you. I appreciated the gesture but I was not going to get back to them.

However, we also had friends who just stopped by briefly with a casserole... baskets of fruits and veggies... thoughtful cards... and flowers. One friend even brought a case of water to make sure Mick was staying hydrated!

They all said the same thing: "I know you don't need this, but I hope you can use it. We just wanted to do something to help and let you know we love you guys."

Wow! Those gifts were better than a million bucks!

People can always eat and flowers can add a little beauty around the house. So you can't go wrong with things like that. Even if you feel like a total cliché showing up with a casserole — make a joke about it — and let them know it's a "casserole of love".

Believe me — the thought along with an action makes a big difference. And you feel good too!

If I felt run down when my kids were little, one of my girlfriends would come over and say, "Hey — give me the kids. I've got them for the day, you go to sleep. I'll bring them back tonight."

WOW. What another great gift — the gift of time!

And to me, the gift of experience is invaluable. You learn so much as you go through life and if you can share those lessons to help others — you're giving an amazing gift.

There are so many people you can help right now. You don't need the perfect circumstances to give. You just have to realize that you have the power to give.

Share wisdom. I know I can help mothers, entrepreneurs, copywriters and women. So I share what I know. And that includes the good... the bad... and the ugly.

Share wealth. Of course, giving money can be extremely beneficial. If there's a cause or charity you really care about —

put your money where your mouth is. Support them financially.

Do what you can. When you can only do a little then do a little. When you can do a lot — dang it — then do a lot. And let me tell you this: Writing a big fat check to your favorite charity is stinkin' AWESOME!

Yes, a 'big fat check' is going to be relative to what you have.

Once upon a time, $100 was a big fat check to me. And when I could do it, I loved doing it.

Then $1,000 became a big fat check... then $10,000 became a big fat check... and eventually $100,000 was a big fat check!

I haven't written a million dollar check yet — but hey, it's a goal!

Try to give your financial gifts anonymously or at least privately. If you're doing it for the accolades or to get a plaque with your name on it — you're missing out on the real spirit of giving.

There is truly more happiness in giving than receiving.

## LESSON #38
### BE A MENTOR WITHOUT THE TITLE.

There's no moment in life when you become a mentor. It's an evolution.

Your life lessons have value and can benefit others undergoing what you've already experienced.

This is an ongoing process in life. You're never done learning, so you're never done teaching either! You don't need the title to be someone's mentor. You become a mentor by the example you set and by the time you're willing to give to help others grow.

People will decide if they want to follow your example or not.

At any stage of life — you are a mentor or a mentee. So don't think you have to possess some magical amount of knowledge or wisdom or skill to teach. Your learning process can be a teaching opportunity for someone who's not as far along as you.

I have a button on my desk that says "Be a mentor. A mentor be." It's a cycle: You give, you learn, you give, you learn.

These days, I'm asked quite often to be a copy mentor. I can't say yes to everyone. Personal mentoring is time consuming and energy draining. But mentoring doesn't have to be a one-on-one experience. For example...

I also mentor by teaching small groups... at seminars... on my Carline Cole YouTube channel... other social media platforms... in my CopyStar ezine... writing books... and on my website www.carlinecole.com . Thanks to the Internet and social media you can get access to mentoring — no matter where you live in the world.

I try to give as much free advice as possible. And I have been criticized for it. For example, one colleague said "You're giving away stuff for free that other copywriting programs are charging an arm and a leg for! You could be making a lot more money if you sold these training programs on your YouTube channel." So why do I do it?

Because I want to.

Copywriting has been very good to me. It's given me a wonderful career and amazing opportunities to travel. It helped take care of my family financially. Sharing my knowledge with up-and-coming writers is my way to give back. And I want to give freely (see Lesson #3).

Sharing what I know with you is not going to take food off my table. You're not competing with me. And there's plenty of work to go around. So why not share?

Plus, I enjoy seeing the next generation of copywriters take what I teach them and make it their own!

I love it when I get an email like the one I got recently from Hamza who lives in Pakistan. He participated in a Cover Test Challenge in my C.R.A.Z.Y Copy System Live Mentoring Show. And his cover test beat out the competitors — and spanked my control! He got to earn while he learned. Here's what he said:

10/21/21

 Hey Carline! Just wanted to thank you for sending the "I'm on a Roll, I Beat Carline's Control" T-shirt and the sample of my promo.

 You have no idea how much confidence I've gotten after winning this challenge. THANK YOU SO FRICKIN MUCH!

 As someone whose first language isn't English, I always had this insecurity that my writing wouldn't resonate with native speakers. This win helped me overcome that fear. You are awesome. I'm glad I have you as a mentor ❤

Best,
Hamza A.

---

So how do you find a mentor? If you flat out ask someone "Will you be my mentor?" You're probably going to get a "No". Like I said, mentoring can be very time and energy consuming. So try this instead:

Ask a potential mentor a specific question. Then follow up and let the mentor know how the advice turned out. Be thankful. Then ask another question and follow up. I call this "Baby Steps to Getting a Mentor!"

Develop a relationship. Ask what they did in a situation you're struggling with. Ask their opinion on an idea you have. Most folks will give you time if you just ask for a bite and not a whole meal!

Clayton Makepeace was my mentor. But I didn't start off by asking him to mentor me.

I studied his copy. When he came to the office at Phillips Publishing, I would ask him one or two questions about something he wrote. He saw that I was serious and interested in his work. That allowed us to develop a friendship.

And then, one day, Clayton said, "Anytime you have a question, feel free to call me." And boy oh boy did I ever! Eventually I asked him to look at my copy and asked for crits. He could see how my writing was improving and he eventually hired me to work as a ghostwriter.

I spent years working and learning from Clayton. And that experience gave me the courage to go after my own clients. Funny thing — while I was learning from Clayton — I was also sharing my knowledge with other younger writers. The cycle was perpetuating.

Be a mentor. A mentor be.

## LESSON #39

### CREATE A THEME FOR EACH NEW YEAR — AND BE TRUE TO IT.

For 2021, the year I wrote this book, my theme was "Grow — even if you must stay planted."

We were still engulfed in the COVID-19 pandemic and I knew that even though I couldn't travel, there would still be opportunities for me to grow if I looked for them.

I've been choosing themes for each year for about 25 years now. I develop my themes by thinking about what I want to accomplish in the upcoming year.

In December, I review the challenges and successes from the previous year and then put together a plan for making the new year even better. I don't call them resolutions. They're guidelines for success. They help me stay focused and not go chasing the "shiny objects" that can distract me.

My friends think I'm extremely spontaneous — ready to jump at any new thing that comes along. But that's not really true. It's actually the opposite.

By having my guidelines and goals for the year — it's easy to make a decision or take advantage of an opportunity. For example, if my goal is to purchase 2 rental properties at a certain price point — it's easy to be "spontaneous" and take advantage of a good deal that comes my way. If the opportunity supports the goal — then I go for it!

But if buying a property is not the goal — then it's easy to pass on the deal without overthinking the decision. It doesn't work with what I'm trying to accomplish this year.

If you're familiar with the Myers-Briggs personality test — I'm an ENFP. That means I can be spontaneous... easily distracted... and prone to multi-tasking. So if I don't anchor myself with my guidelines for the year — I will be all over the place and won't get stuff done.

That's a powerful lesson I'm very glad I learned about myself. It's OK to try new things and be spontaneous — but take care of business first!

Having a theme and clear goals for the year keeps me on track — and that has been a reason for my success.

So as I'm contemplating the new year — I write down the answers to the following questions:

- What are your financial goals?
- What are your emotional goals?
- What are your business goals
- What are your spiritual goals?
- What are your social goals?

I put down at least three answers to each question. By the way, the answers can't be generic like, "I want to be happy" or "make more money". You need to be able to quantify them — so you will be accountable for what you put down.

Here's an example:

My social goal this year was to have a few small, intimate gatherings at our house. Big parties are a breeze for me and I love them! Hosting a hundred people is much easier than having a dinner party of six. Why?

Because I can bounce around between people when there's a huge crowd. A little chit-chat here and there and off I go! If you run into someone annoying — it's easy to take off. It's great!

But when it's an intimate gathering, I have to slow down and be present. Conversations get lengthier and deeper. And if I realize I don't like the people — I'm STUCK! I can't run away like I could in a crowd.

So this goal was to force me to work on this weakness. Plus — having a large gathering was just not an option during a pandemic!

This exercise forces you to take time and review the important parts of your life. Put together specific goals on what you want to accomplish in the next 12 months. You've just created a life schedule.

But don't just put it aside! Review it monthly or quarterly to check in on how you're doing.

Did you have that party for six people? If not — when can you make it happen this month?

Are you saving X amount every month? Yes you are? Great — keep it up! If you're not on schedule — how are you going to catch up before the year ends?

With regular check-ups — there won't be surprises or disappointments at the end of the year. You're actively participating in your life. You're accountable for your life schedule. And you will get it done.

A goal without a plan ain't nothing but a dream.

## LESSON #40

USING PROFANITY DOESN'T MAKE YOU COOL, BIG OR BAD. IT JUST GIVES YOU A POTTY MOUTH.

I honestly don't see the benefit of using profanity.

When we were little, we cursed because we were trying to be cool. But that's a kid thing — it's a totally immature point of view.

The reality is, you're not cool... you're not popular... you've just got a potty mouth!

I hear cursing a lot and I'll be the first to admit I've used it at times. But sometimes I meet people who don't seem to know any other kind of words!

I think, "OMG, can you put a sentence together without one cuss word in there?" And they probably can't!

Maybe it's just that I'm older now, but I think it makes you sound stupid. If you can't have a conversation without using words that are intended to offend or shock people, you have a problem.

If you want to cuss in the privacy of your own home with your "peeps" — that's on you. But don't expose other people to your foul mouth. Your friends may not object to you dropping the F-bomb, but why risk offending others — especially in a professional or business setting?

It's just not necessary and most of the time, it's inappropriate.

A business letter should not include profanity. Consider it a professional challenge to get your message across without offending your market. Try a dang blasted euphemism doggone it!

If you're speaking at a seminar or giving a speech — you can make your message interesting and punchy without profanity. You don't know who's in your audience — so why risk offending them?

And if you say, "Well that's just me. That's how I talk". I say "That's a cop-out! You weren't born with a potty mouth. It's a learned behavior that can be unlearned."

There's enough yucky, dirty stuff going on in the world without your potty mouth adding to the filth.

And if you're a writer — ESPECIALLY if you're a writer — relying on profanity to make your point just makes it look like you can't get the job done on your skills alone.

I'm not saying you can't be edgy — but euphemisms can replace profanity — and you can still engage your audience. You're trying to draw people to your message — so why take the risk of pushing someone away?

If you need a little reminder to nix the dirty words — keep a bar of soap handy to wash your mouth out.

## LESSON #41

### TRAVEL REMINDS ME HOW INSIGNIFICANT I AM TO THE PLANET.

I've learned when you travel for a month — you come home six months more mature. You're in a different environment. You use new skills. You learn from others. And you GROW!

In my travels — I've made amazing connections with people from all over the world. I still keep in touch with many of them.

We have friends from Italy we met over a decade ago. At first we had to use Google Translate to communicate with Luisa and Reno. Their daughter Serena and her friend Monica even lived with us for 3 months to become certified in the English language. And we had the pleasure of attending Serena's amazing Italian wedding — where the food and the fun never stopped.

We made friends with the Maasai tribesmen in Kenya. Eating... talking... and seeing their lives up close and personal had a profound impact on me. Months later, I got an email from Mike — a Maasai Warrior — and it brought back fond memories of an amazing experience.

Traveling teaches you that you don't need much "stuff". If

I'm traveling for a month, I learned to fit my belongings in a carry-on bag. I will have to wash my clothes once or twice, but that's all the "stuff" I need.

And letting go of that stuff becomes a metaphor for life. Clearing out the "baggage" in life that weighs you down is liberating.

Travel also teaches and reminds you that you are in the minority. You have a surplus while most of the world is in a deficit.

The majority of the world does not live like the average American. When you visit a developing country — you see houses made of aluminum sheets and cardboard — and families of 6 or more live in them! And it's not temporary housing — it's their home.

I remember watching one of those reality courtroom TV shows years ago. A Hispanic man was arrested for refusing to vacate a condemned house with no running water and electricity.

When the judge asked him why he refused to leave, his answer was heartbreakingly simple: "The house has walls. It has a roof. It has a floor. This is the best house I ever lived in."

One man's condemned house is another man's castle.

My husband and I did volunteer work with our congregation in rural Kentucky — right here in the USA about 10 years ago. Driving around, I saw shacks and unfinished homes and thought to myself, "There's no way anyone lives here." But then I'd see kids playing out in front... and sure enough, that's their home.

Getting outside of my comfort zone and seeing how people live around the world reminds me of how inconsequential I am. It's eye-opening and humbling.

The sad truth is that much of the poverty that exists is man-made and caused by greed, poorly-run governments and unethical business practices.

Scientists have said the earth produces more than enough food to sustain everyone alive. It's greed, politics and privilege that create the poverty.

Traveling makes me grateful for what I have but it also reminds me to share what I can with others... to use my abilities and capabilities to help the best I can... to not be selfish with natural resources... to not assume it cannot happen to me... and to continue to pray for the real heavenly government that will eradicate poverty, suffering and inequality forever.

## LESSON #42

### GIVE A BIG TIP FOR A LITTLE PURCHASE.

A couple of people in my life have taught me this lesson. The first person was my stepfather, Gerry.

He was a cab driver and I often rode along with him when I wasn't in school. I would sit in the front seat of the cab and start conversations with the fares he picked up.

After the passengers tipped Gerry — many of them would tip me too!

That experience taught me that tips are nice. They let you know that you're doing a good job. But for people working in the service industry, tips are much more than that.

Tips are a big chunk of their income. That's why Gerry was extremely generous when he tipped another service person. He would buy a cup of coffee for 25 cents and leave a dollar tip.

He over-tipped so much that my mom taught us kids to pick up half the tips Gerry left.

She would argue with him and say, "We're not rich! We can't afford to tip like that!" But Gerry did it anyway. He knew the value of a good tip.

My copywriting mentor, Clayton Makepeace was another

big tipper. He grew up poor and respected the work of the Average Joe. He knew they would never make the kind of money he did. Clayton was especially fond of servers and musicians.

I once saw him tip $100 for a $10 purchase.

And if the music was sounding good — he would make the musician's night with a big, fat, eye-popping tip. Clayton was never big on donating to organized charities — but he kept many service industries afloat — especially during tough financial times with his generous and regular tips.

Those are just two of the many examples of big tippers in my life. And I wanted to imitate them. I looked for ways to give big — even if I wasn't "living large".

I started paying the toll on the highway for the person behind me — just because. I left a nice note along with gift cards to my mail carrier, UPS and FedEx delivery folks. I would treat a random stranger to lunch without them knowing it was me. It was just fun and it felt good.

Recently I was on a road trip driving through North Carolina, USA. And let me tell you, the rest stops were disgusting. I thought I would have to hold it in until we got to another state. But we pulled into one rest stop and it was spotless! It smelled clean. Floors were mopped. Toilet bowl sparkled! Wow!

I made it a point to find an employee. When I saw the older gentleman with the mop, I asked him, "Do you take care of this restroom?" He said humbly, "Yes, ma'am, I do". So I reached in my pocket and took out the only cash I had on me. It was just $5. I gave it to him and thanked him for taking pride in his work and doing such a great job. The smile on his face was priceless.

Not only can a nice tip make a big difference to the person who receives it — that tip makes you feel good too! You get a rush of feel-good hormones from your brain when you do nice things for people.

In the United States, we have a strong tipping culture. We know that service people rely on tips for their income. So even if someone doesn't do a great job, you should still leave a decent tip. For example, it may not be their fault if your meal is late or there's a delay with valet parking.

If someone takes the time to get to know me, talks to me and delivers a great service — these days I will find a way to make sure I tip that person a whole lot more than they were expecting.

It's even more important in countries where the value of a dollar is high. Don't think in their currency — think in yours. When we were in Sri Lanka, I realized that a $1 tip was equal to someone's income for three or four days. It was the same thing in Madagascar. So instead of giving them an equivalent tip based on their currency — give that US dollar or more!

Your dollar may be a million bucks or a lifesaver. You just never know.

## LESSON #43

DON'T BE ASHAMED OF WHERE YOU CAME FROM.
USE YOUR PAST TO LAUNCH YOUR FUTURE.

Your childhood was out of your control (Lesson #9).

You had nothing to do with your birth, or who your parents were, or where you lived or how you were raised. So do not be ashamed of where you came from.

If you got the short end of the stick early in life, don't dwell on it. And don't stay bitter about it. Try to find the good that came from the difficulty or negativity.

Did a negligent parent teach you at an early age to be independent? Did that early independence set you up to become an entrepreneur? Did poverty create a fire in your belly to succeed financially? Did the bad examples in your life teach you what not to imitate?

You can find something good in bad stuff that happens. Own your story.

Use your upbringing as a launching pad. Your future does not have to be dictated by your past.

If you are determined to make a difference in your life... to improve your situation... to change your story — you can do it.

Don't miss out on opportunities in your present by dwelling

in the past. Give yourself permission to say "What happened to me as a kid SUCKED. But I'm an adult now and I have the power to take control of my life."

I never got to know my biological father. He didn't want to be in my life. He wanted to terminate me as an embryo. I used to feel really sad about that. Then I realized I need to thank that guy for his DNA. There are some things I know I didn't inherit from my mom. So I have to assume it came from him.

He didn't want to be around me because he thought I was a terrible person. He wasn't around long enough to even know me.

And then I took it one step further. I felt sorry for him. He missed out on getting to raise an AMAZING daughter who turned into a heck of an AWESOME woman! Poor guy. His loss.

Remember: Every obstacle you experience — there's someone with similar circumstances who prevails. You be that winner. Race... gender... poverty... or abuse doesn't have to define whether you will be successful or not.

Don't let yourself miss out on what life has to offer you because you keep dwelling on what life handed you at birth.

I know people who still complain about how they had terrible parents. They act like all this stuff happened yesterday. Yet they're in their 40s... 50s... and 60s. Get therapy to help you if you're stuck in the past.

You can only control what happens going forward. It's within your power to make a great life for yourself. So forgive who you need to forgive so you take away the power they have over you.

Depression is living in the past. Anxiety is living in the future. Happiness is the present.

## LESSON #44
SHOWING HUMILITY TAKES COURAGE.

I'm still learning this.

Humility is not a weakness... it's a strength.

Sometimes the strongest thing you can do is just to be quiet — even when you're right — and this is very hard for me!

I'm an extrovert. I want to speak up. I have NO problem jumping into the mix to give my opinion on matters.

But the strongest people I know are mild-mannered... quiet... soft-spoken. Their humility makes them powerful.

You become a better person when you can be quiet and listen to critiques about yourself.

If somebody is going to tell you something you don't want to hear but you know that person is coming from a good place — you need to be quiet and listen. You need to be humble and really think about what they're saying to you.

You don't see your flaws like other people see them. You minimize them without realizing how they affect others.

It's a punch in the gut to hear something you don't like. But be quiet. Be humble. Hear the intention behind the words.

Here's an example. When I was about 25, a friend of mine said to me one day, "You talk too much."

I blew it off, like, "Of course I talk too much! I'm an extrovert, I love talking!"

And she said, "NO. You... talk... too... much. You need to be quiet and LISTEN when it's someone else's turn to talk."

Well dang. That floored me. I knew I talked a lot, but I couldn't see the difference between being talkative and talking over people.

Her point was not that I should stop being outgoing, but that I should shut up... listen to what the other person has to say... and THEN comment.

I kept wanting to jump in before she finished talking. I assumed I already knew what she was going to say and I wanted to make my own point! I might have been right, but I wasn't respecting my friend by interrupting her. And she was right!

I love fast-paced conversation. But she was slow at getting her thoughts together. I thought I was helping her by finishing her sentences. But she didn't need my help. She knew what she wanted to say. She just needed more time to get it out. And I needed to listen and not cut her off.

It took a lot of courage for her to tell me that and I deeply appreciate the friendship. I had to develop humility to see her point of view.

I even asked her for help. I told her to give me a little cue when I was running over her in conversation. When she did, I became aware of it. And I could see what she meant.

Another example happened during my internship at Q107 radio station in Washington D.C. during my senior year of college. I worked in the advertising department and got to sit in a creative meeting to brainstorm new projects. I spoke up several times but after every comment I made, I giggled.

After the meeting, one of the accountants attending the meeting pulled me aside.

He said, "Carline, you made some good suggestions in the meeting. But you negated everything you said with that silly giggle. You need to stop it. You're not a kid. Say what you need to say and stand behind it. Don't use that giggle as a childish way to give you an out."

OMG! I was so embarrassed.

I was thinking... "Who IS this guy? He doesn't know me!"

I wanted to run away and hide. He could tell I was embarrassed but he didn't let me off the hook. All I could say was, "OK, thank you. I'll work on it." But steam was coming out of my ears as I walked away.

I had to swallow my pride. I thought about the counsel. And then I saw that he was right. I did have a nervous giggle. It was a defense mechanism. If I spoke up and said something that was actually dumb, well (giggle, giggle) I was just kidding. You shouldn't have taken me seriously in the first place!

What a light bulb moment! The accountant didn't have to pull me aside to share his observation. But I'm so glad he did. His advice gave me a heads up in the business world. It was a valuable insight. And I'm so grateful he took the time to tell me.

Throughout my career, I've seen many other women do the "giggle" thing. Some much older than I was at 20.

When I can, I try to pay back the favor and pull them aside too.

## LESSON #45

### IF YOU GIVE ME A GIFT THAT SAYS "ASSEMBLY REQUIRED" — YOU ARE NOT MY FRIEND.

I do not want gifts that require me to put them together. I'm not going to do it. And the gift will end up in the closet or tucked away somewhere and never see the light of day!

If it's something you really want me to have — then take the extra step and give me the finished product.

If you know a little 5-year-old girl wants a bike — would you give it to her in a box, hand her a screwdriver and say "Have at it"? No! That would be mean. Well, think of me as that 5-year-old when it comes to assembly-required gifts.

The real gift is riding the bicycle, not getting a box full of parts.

If you don't know what to give me, that's fine! You don't have to give me *anything*.

But if you really want to give me a gift — don't make me work for it! Do not give me stuff I have to find a place for. Give me disposable gifts. Tickets to a theater... flowers... or a dinner date. At this stage of my life — I want experiences and not things.

My daughter #2 struggles to find an anniversary gift for me

and her dad. She says daughter #1 has it easy because all she has to do is give us something our grandsons made and we're over-the-moon happy. And that's so true!

So I told daughter #2 to stop trying so hard. We don't need anything. So for our 38$^{th}$ anniversary, she found a photo of me and Mick in the waiting room of the hospital. My husband was going in for a procedure and it was a scary time. I snapped a photo of the two of us, wearing face masks while waiting for Mick's name to be called. I sent the photo to my kids to give them an update.

She took that photo and added a little design to it that said "Happy 38$^{th}$ Anniversary Mom and Dad. Love Tiara."

When we got that photo — all sorts of emotions surfaced. She summed up for us what Year 38 was about. The endless doctor visits and the unknown. It also reminded us of how far we've come. That picture was the absolute best gift she could've given us. And we have it framed and placed right next to the hand drawings from our grandsons!

The gift took daughter #2 about 5 minutes to create and cost her nothing. But to us, it's priceless.

No assembly required.

## LESSON #46
### IT'S ONLY EASY WHEN YOU KNOW HOW.

Isn't it amazing when you see someone create a work of art that is gorgeous — and when you compliment them on the impressive masterpiece — they say, "Oh that? It's so easy!"

That's when I say, "It's only easy when you know how."

Now, I love to crochet baby blankets and scarves. It's so easy for me. But none of my friends crochet — so they are really impressed with my work.

But when it comes to copywriting, the reverse seems to be true. People read my copy and say, "Man, your writing is so simple. I can do this."

That's when I tell them, "Go ahead!"

Because I know it's only easy when you know how.

When you master your skill, you make the job look effortless. But to master that skill, you've got to practice... Practice... and PRACTICE! And it can take thousands of hours to make it look easy.

I want to make my copy as conversational as I possibly can.

I read it out loud. I have other copywriters review my work...

I get my friends to read the copy out loud. If they stumble over a word, I replace the word — not my friend. I want my copy to flow like a buttery river!

I look at the cadence of the words. I make sure I have the right syllables that create a natural beat and rhythm to the sound of my copy.

I go over and over my copy to make sure it "feels" right.

All of those things go into my 'easy writing', my 'simple style' that a fifth-grader could read with no problem.

How do you explain a complicated brain nutrient like "phosphatidylserine" in a few seconds — so you can keep your reader's attention? You break it down phonetically — "foss-fah-tie-doll-sir-een" — and then give it a nickname, like "PS" — for short.

How do you write headlines that create intrigue and curiosity in your readers, so they want to know more? You snag their attention with an urgent problem like "Can't Go?" or "Got Bad Breath?" or even "What to do when your blood pressure won't go down."

How do you write a lead that stops people in their tracks because they just HAVE to know more about your promotion? You start that lead sentence with, "What I'm about to reveal may shock you..."

Figuring that stuff out is work. A lot of work. It's years of trial and error. It's doing and Doing and DOING until you're done!

UConn basketball player Gabby Williams says: "We make it look easy on the court, because we practice until we cannot get it wrong anymore." I keep that quote above my desk to remind me to keep practicing.

I want people to tell me my copy looks SOOOO easy — because that means I'm still practicing and getting better at my craft — even though I've been a freelance copywriter for over 22 years.

Clayton Makepeace used to turn in the most amazing copy. One day I asked him, "How do you make this look so easy?"

That's when he told me "Don't compare my sixteenth draft to your first draft. It takes a lot of work to make it look this easy." I have never forgotten that lesson.

When you can make your copy look seamless — you are headed to A-List copywriter level. But it's only easy when you know how.

## LESSON #47

### AFTER A TRIAL, YOU CAN EITHER BE BETTER OR BITTER.

A minister named Bryon Carlson taught me this lesson.

We all undergo trials in life. If you're alive — you will have trials and tribulations. If you're not experiencing one right now — rest up. It's coming.

But no matter who you are, you will always have two choices that are within your control. You can either be better or bitter from the trial.

If somebody was in an accident and lost one arm, that person could become bitter about that missing arm. Or they could become better by being thankful they didn't lose both arms.

Another example is when a couple experiences a miscarriage.

If you've been trying for years and then miscarry, you can be very bitter — "Why am I the one who lost my baby? There are so many women having kids and they can't even take care of them."

If you feel like you only had one opportunity to have that

baby, it's extremely painful. So it's easy to become bitter. But you can also look to become better.

You can say to yourself, "Well, I experienced being pregnant. I know my body can get pregnant. I experienced a lot of joy in my pregnancy. I'm sad that I lost this baby. But I have hope for the future. I can try again."

Now I don't mean to minimize the loss. I don't mean that you can't go through your grieving process for as long as you need. And I don't mean to sound harsh or uncaring. However, ultimately you have to choose between better or bitter.

When my daughter #1 miscarried in her first trimester, it was a loss for the entire family. When she was ready to remember the baby, she decided to get a special ring with a November birthstone — the month the baby was due. She wears that ring often. Most people just think it's a beautiful ring. But she knows the real importance of it. And it's a reminder that she will get to meet that baby one day soon in Paradise.

Find something to give you a better outlook so you don't get stuck in bitterness.

You can find something to make you better from any trial or tribulation you go through. The question is "Are you willing to look for it?"

It's easier to be bitter, to sink in the mire of your misfortune. But it takes inner strength and fortitude to choose to see each day as a new opportunity, to look at the positive and GO for it. When you do, your life will be so much better.

At every moment in life, you have that choice between better or bitter. You can give it away, but no one can take it away from you.

## LESSON #48

DON'T HATE YOUR BODY PARTS. THEY'RE DOING THE BEST THEY CAN WITH WHAT YOU FEED THEM.

Whatever you feed your body is what you're made of.

If you're mad because you have big thighs or thick ankles or a round belly or weak bones or poor eyesight — they're a result of choices you made in caring for your body your entire life.

Yes, there's a level of genetics in play, that's true — but what you eat is by far the most important influence on how your body looks and functions.

People hate their bodies because they don't like what they see. But you put that stuff there.

Your body is programmed to LIVE! It's constantly trying to stay in a state of homeostasis — a natural balance — to keep you healthy. If you knock it off balance with bad eating habits, it's going to become harder to get back to that equilibrium — especially as you get older.

And your body will start to sacrifice less important parts to save what MUST survive.

For example: If you have poor circulation, your hands and your feet stay cold. Why? Because your body's trying to draw the slow-moving blood to vital organs — like your heart and brain. You can lose a couple of fingers and toes and survive. But lose heart or brain function — and you're kaput.

Your body also has the power to self-heal. Think of something as simple as a paper cut. Even if you ignore it, it's going to heal. Your body sends all kinds of signals — to stop the blood flow, to attack any invading bacteria and to generate new tissue to seal the wound.

Most of the damage happens because of what you put in your body. Food is fuel. So, is it going to be an apple or an apple pie?

The apple will feed your body nutrients to fight disease, boost immune health and satisfy hunger. The apple pie might taste good momentarily, but it's breaking down cell function... wreaking havoc with your blood sugar... and speeding the aging process.

The choice is yours and you don't have to get it right all the time. Your body is forgiving but it does have a breaking point and that's called disease.

And by the way, you can always just change your attitude! If you have big hips, you could lose some weight and they might go down a bit, but if they're big, so be it. That's genetics and you can't change your skeletal system.

But you know what? You can change the style of clothes you wear so they flatter your body type. Or heck, just embrace your big hips! What you hate, others envy. I promise you there are people out there who will say, "Wow! I wish I had hips like that." I'm one of them!

I don't have big hips and I always wanted them. My mom used to joke and say if I put a kid on my hip, he would just slide right off and hit the ground. Nothing there for him to hold on to. So I'm envious of nice curves.

## LESSON #48

When I was 9 months pregnant with daughter #2, my measurements were 40-40-40. I cried and told my husband I looked like a rectangle! But that body delivered a healthy 9-pound, 6.5 ounce baby — so that rectangle did the job!

Take care of your body so it can take care of you.

## LESSON #49

### COMPLIMENT GENEROUSLY. CRITICIZE STINGILY — UNLESS IT'S COPY CRITS.

Be generous with your compliments. Even if you have something negative to say, start with kind words.

A compliment can bring a smile and lift the spirit. So look for ways to compliment the people in your life every day. Be specific with your compliments. "You look nice" is OK. But even better is... "That color looks great on you!" "You are ROCKIN' that outfit!" "Keep up the good work in losing weight — I can really see your progress!" "That was very kind of you to help your sister with her homework."

You don't need an "event" to give a compliment. And compliments are not a limited resource — so give them freely.

Make your words sincere. Let the person know what you're about to say is because you respect, appreciate or love them.

I've learned the opposite is true about criticism. Be very stingy with them. Criticism — if not given properly — can easily backfire and cause hurt and resentment.

So before you even open your mouth to criticize, ask yourself "Is it worth it? Do you need to bring this matter up? Will it benefit the person? Do they really need to know?"

Many times, it's not that big a deal. And you can just chalk it up to imperfection or the person having a bad day. If so, leave it alone. Don't criticize people because *you* need to get something off *your* chest.

But if the matter does need to be brought up and you're the person to say something — then be tactful. Find an appropriate time and place to share your concern. Do not make the person feel attacked or shamed.

If I see a potential harm coming to someone I care about, I will speak up. If they're going to hurt themselves physically, emotionally, spiritually or financially — I will bring it to their attention.

I will risk the friendship to bring up the issue because if I don't — I'm not really a friend.

You can use words like, "There's something I want to share with you... " or, "You may not be aware of this, but when you..."

I also like to use what I call "permission-based criticism". It's a way to prepare the person for what's about to come.

My most famous line is, "You know I love you, right?"

When my friends hear those words from me, they know I need to share a sensitive matter with them. It's my way of asking permission before I say something they might not want to hear.

If I ask someone's permission and they say "No, I don't want to hear it" — OK. I won't say it. I'll move on. But if they say "Yes, tell me," I will speak up.

Everything I've just said is about giving personal critiques. But when it comes to business and giving copy crits — well that's a whole different ball game!

With copy crits — my job is to bring up as many flaws as I can find and highlight even the tiny errors in the copy. You may see so much red ink on the page that it looks like a crime scene!

I will tear up the copy... break it down... and give it back to you to rebuild.

One of my copy cubs once sent me a stamp that says "LAME!" in big red letters. That was the one word I consistently used when editing his copy.

But along with the stamp, he included a note to say, "Carline, I just want you to know how much I appreciate your crits. I got a new control! And it's because you weren't afraid to tell me where my copy was lame."

So when it comes to copy crits, I go for the jugular — and do whatever it takes to create KILLER copy.

But even then — I make sure the intent is clear. That's why I said in Lesson #34 — before I start a copy critique session — I share my mantra:

"You're wonderful. You're awesome. Your copy sucks — you don't!"

## LESSON #50
### I LOVE MY KIDS BUT I NEED MY SANITY.

I loved motherhood. I still love motherhood! But I also realized that it is just one part of my life.

I was a full-time, stay-at-home mom the first three years of motherhood. I had a 2½ year old and a 1 year-old. It didn't take long for me to figure out motherhood couldn't be my entire life. I needed to do other things. I wanted to do other things.

I was gonna go crazy if I didn't have other outlets that didn't include my children. And having a crazy mom wasn't going to help anybody!

I remember one particularly horrific day. Both kids had gotten on my last nerve. I was done. I knew my husband would be home from work soon — so I just waited near the front door. As soon as he opened the door, I dropped the baby in his arms and handed him the toddler.

I said, "I gotta get out of here. I'm going to K-Mart."

I needed adult conversation. I needed stimulation. I needed to feel like I could do something more than just wipe butts and stick a boob in a kid's mouth.

I saw many of my friends embrace motherhood and make it their life and identity. And that's fine if that's what they wanted. But that was not me. I love my kids but I NEED my sanity.

My goal was to raise my kids so that they can grow up, move out and become independent adults.

After my K-Mart meltdown, I arranged with my friend Maria, who had kids around the same age as mine to have 'mommy swaps'. Maria would bring her kids to my house for the morning and have some time to herself. Then the next time, my kids would go to her place and I'd get a break.

My breaks usually included writing articles to submit for magazine publication... sewing... volunteer work with my congregation... or sleeping!

Now that I have grandkids, I know how important it is for their mom to get a break. So I offer 'mommy breaks' as often as I can. Recently the kids spent a week with us. When I asked my daughter what she did with her free time she said, "Nothing! It was GREAT!"

And sometimes nothing is exactly what you need.

I've also learned that maintaining your sanity is not only important when the kids are young.

It's important when they're grown too.

Adult children can suck the life out of you if you let them.

Be careful not to take on the baggage of your adult children. They will make decisions you don't agree with. You have to respect their boundaries as independent adults.

I've learned to ask what they need. Do they want my advice or just want to vent? Are they asking me as their mom or as a friend?

I don't solve their problems for them. But I can hear them out. I can offer my experience. And I'm going to pray and trust they will figure things out for themselves.

And I can always encourage them to take advantage of the Therapy Fund in Lesson #22 when needed.

## LESSON #51

### SHOW UP EARLY AND YOU'RE TWO-THIRDS OF THE WAY TO REACHING YOUR GOAL.

This is a fundamental life skill.

The sooner you can learn this lesson — the more successful you'll be in anything you set out to accomplish. Anything! Just show up early and be present in body and mind.

If your job starts at 9 o'clock — you're not "on time" if you show up at 9 o'clock. You're late. Get to work at least 15 minutes early. That gives you time to get changed into your uniform... put your stuff away... get your coffee... or go to the bathroom — so when 9 o'clock comes — you are *working*.

Show up early and you've won two-thirds of the battle.

Make getting to work early part of your work ethics. It shows you respect and appreciate your job. It shows you take your job seriously. It gives you a good reputation. It also makes you available for unexpected opportunities.

I've gotten jobs just because I was the first person in the office that day.

I may not have been the best person for the job — but I was there. For example, back in 1987, I was a part-time customer service rep at Phillips Publishing, a young, entrepreneurial direct-response marketing company. One day I had gotten to work 30 minutes early and was in the lunchroom eating a bagel.

My manager came in and looked a bit frantic. The order processing team was short-staffed and getting swamped with mail orders. She needed extra order processors. Well, that wasn't my job, I didn't know how to do it but when she asked me to help, I said, "Sure, I'm a fast learner." It was an opportunity to learn a new skill and to become more valuable to the company.

I learned the process in just a few hours. So from then on, any time they needed help in the mail room, my manager would take me off the phones to help.

Now — anybody who was sitting in that lunchroom eating a bagel that day would've gotten that opportunity. But it was me. And it happened because I was early.

It's a small example but it meant that I was no longer just a customer service rep. I now had order processing experience. And guess what? I got a raise because of that new skill and ability. What's more, when the company had to downsize the teams, I kept my job. I was more valuable to the company because I was cross-trained in two departments.

Two years later, I wanted to apply for a job in the marketing department. When the new department called my manager for a reference, one of the things my manager said was "She's a fast learner and she shows up early for work."

I certainly didn't have the skills for the marketing job but they took a chance on me because of my reputation. And thank goodness for that — because that marketing job led me on the path to becoming the A-List direct-response copywriter I am today.

When you show up early — opportunities appear.

## LESSON #52

### AN OPEN HAND RECEIVES MORE THAN A CLOSED FIST.

If you have an opportunity to share — whether it's your time, your money, your knowledge — choose generosity every time.

Open up and do it. You will be better off because no matter how much you give away — you get so much more in return.

That is not only in business. It's in every part of life. I have seen it happen time and time again. And it's never about the amount you have — it's what you do with what you have.

Look for ways to give, and to give unselfishly. Don't give with the motive of getting something in return — it's not tit for tat. But if somebody needs your help and it's within your power to help. Then think like Nike® and Just Do It.

Yes, you need to have some boundaries. But if you can make somebody's life better without harming yourself — then do it.

Let me give you an example. In March 2021, I started a YouTube channel (https://www.youtube.com/c/CarlineCole). My goal is to deliver quality video training for aspiring copywriters. My team and I have worked hard to make the videos valuable. One of the video series is the epic Clayton Makepeace Tribute — where 18 A-List copywriters and marketers share their powerful lessons learned from Clayton. This is copywriting gold, it's available to anyone who wants to watch it on my channel — and it's free.

In the first 8 months, I put up over 150 copywriting training videos on the channel. And I've received dozens and dozens of comments from industry leaders who say the same thing: "I can't believe you're just giving this information away for free."

But what they don't realize is what I have received in return is more valuable than money.

Emails from stay-at-home moms thanking me for the opportunity to learn a skill while their kids take naps. Men and women who love to write but didn't know this "copywriting thing" even existed! Financially strapped folks who are studying every single video... putting the instructions to work... and now making money in copywriting.

I've seen my YouTube channel transform lives.

And a funny thing happened along the way.

Those folks who feast on the free stuff now want MORE! So they sign up for my C.R.A.Z.Y Copy System Live Mentoring Show to earn while they learn directly from me (https://members.carlinecole.com/ready-to-join).

They purchase my e-books from my website ( https://carlinecole.com/carlines-estore/) and they get $950 of my killer swipe file for free when they purchase my book, *"My Life as a 50+ Year-Old White Male: How a Mixed-Race Woman Stumbled Into Direct-Response Copywriting and Succeeded!"* — available at https://bit.ly/mylifebyCarline

Being generous is a great way to do business. It's a great way to live. It doesn't take anything away from you. It might not change your life much, but it can make a huge difference to someone who needs a helping hand.

## LESSON #53

### MAKE PEOPLE BETTER OFF IN WAYS THEY DESIRE — AND ARE WILLING TO PAY FOR.

Bob King, my boss at Phillips Publishing taught me this lesson. It was the mantra of our very successful company.

Bob was a brilliant marketer. He made it very clear to everyone in the company that our job was to make people better off in ways they desire.

In other words, don't offer your market things they don't want or need! It's a much harder sell to convince prospects they need a power tool with 25 features when they know a simple screwdriver works!

Bob taught me to treat my market like a spoiled child: Find out what they want and give it to them!

*Are your joints hurting you? Well, take a look at this amazing nutrient....*

*Can't sleep? Here's a remedy that will put you out like a light...*

*Want to slow down the aging process? Then check out this miracle molecule that erases 10 years off your age...*

In a nutshell: The best way to sell is to listen to what your prospects want. Regurgitate their desires back to them. Provide the solution so they get what they want!

Later on, after about 10 years running the company, Bob added the second part of his mantra: That our customers had to be willing to pay for what they were getting!

He did this to emphasize that you can do a lot of things to help people be better off — but if you can't make a living from that service — you can't help them for very long.

This is still a business. We need to provide valuable solutions and charge a fair price. The customer receives great value for their money and we generate revenue so the business can thrive.

This mantra made Phillips Publishing into a HUGELY successful company, making hundreds of millions of dollars before it was sold.

I kept this mantra in mind when I launched my freelance copywriting business over 22 years ago. It reminds me to work with clients who produce reputable products and deliver excellent customer service.

Then I can do my job to bring them the customers who want to be better off in ways they desire and are very willing to pay for.

## LESSON #54

WRITE LIKE YOU TALK. I BELIEVE THIS IS THE #1 REASON I'M A SUCCESSFUL COPYWRITER.

When I write my copy — I'm having a conversation in print.

I communicate on a very basic, emotional level. I keep it simple. I believe this one sentence — "Write like you talk" — is the reason for my success in this industry.

Clayton Makepeace drilled this into my brain. Whenever I wrote copy, he'd ask, "Who the heck are you talking to? What are you trying to say?"

He would then say "Talk to me. Talk with me. Don't talk at me. Write like you talk, Carline!"

So I do!

I write like I talk, no matter whose "voice" I am writing in.

I've attended numerous seminars where copywriting experts talk about the importance of the voice of your guru. They claim you need to use their personality and nuances in their speech so you can connect well with your prospect. I used to believe that stuff.

But then I realized that if I'm writing copy for five different gurus — males and females, different ages and backgrounds —

and I'm writing like I talk for all of them — then is it REALLY their voice?

I think it's the copywriter's voice! My style of writing and words connect to the prospect. The individuality of the guru is just the icing on the cake! Here's the proof:

Several years ago, I had a very successful control for a client. One day he called and said he and the doctor guru for the product decided to part ways.

My client was upset because we had a strong control that he didn't think we could mail anymore because it was so focused on the doctor. He thought we needed to have a whole new package with the new doctor he just signed up.

I said, "Wait — before we go through the time and expense of creating a new promotion that may or may not work — let's just do this..."

I swapped out the doctors' photos and bio. I did a search and replace to remove or update the info to fit the new doctor. It took about an hour to make these edits. I did not touch the message in the copy. I didn't change the headline. Didn't change the lead. Didn't change squat about the marketing of the product.

Then we mailed out the promo. And you know what happened?

NOTHING!

That's right — nothing changed with the results! The promo continued to be a success.

The copy was strong. It was my voice as a copywriter who got the message in front of the market. The guru was just the face of the product. And changing one face for another made no difference because the desire for the product or promise was strong.

And that package? It's still kicking butt in the mail today!

Since that experience — I've done the doctor switcheroo many times. Haven't been disappointed with the results yet!

Writing like I talk is my secret weapon. But I'm going to share how you can do it too. Ready?

Read your copy out loud.

I'm not kidding! You HAVE to do this. When you read your words out loud — you can hear if you're talking or if you're writing. You can tell if you're having a conversation or if you're reading an article. You can tell if the words resonate or if they sound like an annoying gong!

When you've got your copywriter hat on — you know what you want to say. You know where you want to put the emphasis on your words. But guess what? Your prospect doesn't know any of that!

I get my 12-year old grandson #1 to read my copy out loud to me. I don't prep him in advance. I just want to hear how the words sound. I want to hear where he stumbles. If he doesn't recognize a word or has to re-read a sentence — I find simpler words and fix the stumbling blocks in the copy.

Write to a fifth grade level... or lower!

You don't lose people when you use simple words — but you will lose them with big words they don't understand.

Copywriting is a conversation in print. So just talk to me — and keep it simple, sweetie!

## LESSON #55

### USE YOUR WORDS WISELY. THEY CAN HURT MORE THAN BULLETS.

If you believe the saying *"Sticks and stones may break my bones but words will never hurt me"* — then you're not a writer. At least not a good one.

Words can motivate... inspire... delight... and hurt.

As a copywriter — I see the power of words every day. I see words give people hope... direction... guidance... and even salvation. It's my job to craft words into appealing stories that get the prospect to believe and make that purchase.

But learning the craft also taught me that words can be more powerful and lethal than bullets.

So you have to use your words carefully.

Using the right words is important in all your relationships — but especially with children. You want your words to build them up — not tear them down.

Our kids weren't allowed to say the "S word" when they were young. And in our house, the "S word" was "stupid".

They actually thought it was a curse word — until they got older and figured out the *other* "S word".

Calling people names or calling them stupid — it's just hurtful.

Words are also contextual. A word's meaning can depend on who's using it. How they're using it. When they're using it. What tone they're using. And who they're saying it to.

So use your words wisely. You have two eyes, two ears, but only one mouth.

Watch what you say. Listen to what you hear. And *then* speak. Once hurtful words come out of your mouth, you can apologize — but the damage can still remain.

I heard this story when I was a teenager and it remains a powerful lesson for me:

An old man gave a young boy a bag of nails and told him to hammer them into a newly painted white wooden fence. It took the boy hours to put those nails in the fence.

Once he finished, the old man said, "OK, now go back and carefully pull all the nails out without damaging the fence."

The boy did it. But he told the old man the beautiful fence now had holes and chips from where he removed the nails. Then the old man explained: "Words are like those nails. If you hurt somebody with your words, you can say you're sorry. But it still leaves scars behind."

So bite your tongue. Is what you're about to say really worth it? If not, let it pass.

If you must speak up, pick the right time and think carefully before you speak.

Be careful of absolute words like "always" or "never". If you tell someone "You ALWAYS do this" and they can think of just one time when they didn't — then your statement is negated almost immediately.

That's why I tell my husband when he uses those words when we argue, he's "always wrong and never right."

If you're a writer — especially a direct-response copywriter — you have an even higher level of accountability with your words. You know the power of your words and you have an unfair advantage in how to use them.

## LESSON #56

ASK YOURSELF, "WHAT WOULD A GREAT _____ DO? (EXAMPLE: COPYWRITER, MOM, WIFE, FRIEND). THEN DO IT!

I keep a sticky note above my desk that says "What would a great copywriter do?" It's been there for decades.

I look at it when I get stuck and need inspiration. It allows me to step outside of myself and look for guidance.

Whenever you need help, motivation, or clarity, ask yourself this question. Fill in the noun that fits your situation and you will be surprised how often you get an answer.

You can use this one sentence to help you make decisions in life — in business, family, health — whatever area you need help with.

Let other people's wisdom help you. For example, a chef may spend years mastering a special dish. But if you want to make that meal for dinner — you don't have to go through all the same trials and errors. Just get the recipe and make that meal! Ta dah!

"What would a great _____ do?" is like a little 'cheat sheet' for life!

Here's how I use it. Let's say I'm having a problem with

launching a new health promo. I'm just stuck! I can't figure out the angle and I'm frustrated as heck.

I look up at the note above my desk, and say, "What would a great copywriter do? What would Clayton Makepeace do?"

And then it dawns on me: *He would go after the USP.*

Clayton would focus on the product's "Unique Selling Proposition". He would zone in on what sets the product apart from anything else — and then he would use emotional copy to get the reader hooked. That's what Clayton Makepeace would do.

So now I know what I gotta do too!

OK — now you try it!

Let's say you're dealing with an issue with your child. That kid is getting on your last nerve. Pause and say "What would a great mother do?"

Bring that person to mind and imagine what she would do in your situation.

*Hmm... first she would give her child a hug and say, "I love you." She would make the child feel safe. Then she would calmly address the problem.*

So now — that's what you gotta do too!

Take yourself out of the equation and put in someone who is more equipped or qualified to handle the situation.

You're not making impulsive decisions because this process takes some time to contemplate. It takes the pressure off because you don't have to know all the answers all the time.

I'm not kidding. This REALLY works. It's a powerful lesson for your life arsenal.

I know I don't have all the answers. Being 60 means I'm OK with that too.

## LESSON #57

DO NOT COME TO MY FUNERAL. YOU ARE NOT INVITED. HAVE A "FUN-ERAL" INSTEAD AND ENJOY THE MOMENTS WE SHARED.

My husband and I get into big arguments about this subject a lot. He has these grand plans for his funeral. I just shake my head and say, "I hope I die first."

I don't want any services. I don't want any crying. I don't want anything. If there's ever any doubt — now it's officially recorded in this book! Do NOT give me a funeral.

I'm dead! And to me, death is a comma, not a period.

I'm just taking a long nap. Why make a big deal about a nap? I will wake up again in the resurrection. So the idea of bringing people together to mourn is just yucky to me.

If you want to mourn, do it alone or in a small group so you can support each other. Not in a huge public place — or even on Zoom!

Now look, I get it — a funeral is for the living — not the dead. It can help family members experience closure and get support. So if you need it — then OK. Thank goodness I won't be around to see it!

What I really want is for my loved ones to have a "fun-eral" instead! A celebration of life.

Get together and talk about the wonderful times we shared. Tell crazy stories. Laugh about embarrassing and funny moments. That's part of the healing process too. And I would love that much more than having you at a funeral home or gravesite surrounded by a bunch of other people crying their eyes out.

Please do that for me.

So if I die and you're really, REALLY my friend — please don't come to a funeral my husband decides to have against my will.

Go visit my family instead. Show up a few weeks or months later when everyone else has gone back to their normal lives. That's the time my husband, children and grandchildren will need your support. Come then. Show up then. Be my friend then.

My grandmother used to say, "If you're going to give me flowers, give 'em to me while I'm alive. Then you can put a Post-It Note on my casket that says "I already gave flowers when she could enjoy them!" Mama-Da was cremated — but she would've had a LOT of Post-It Notes on her casket!

So don't come and fill up a funeral home with flowers. Yes I love flowers — but they won't be for me. I'm dead, remember?

## LESSON #58
TREAT YOUR FRIENDS LIKE A BOARD OF DIRECTORS.

I've learned to view myself as the president of the "Carline Anglade-Cole Company" — the business of my life.

A smart company president does not assume she knows everything. She's got a Board of Directors to support her. And they include:

A Chief Financial Officer to handle the money...

... a Chief Operations Officer to handle the daily functions of the business...

... and a Chief Marketing Officer to handle the customers...

If you own a company — you rely on the expertise of your Board of Directors to get the job done. Well, it's no different in your personal life.

You can tap into the expertise of your family and friends to help you run your life smoothly.

But here's a mistake I often see: Many people treat their spouse as the sole member of their Board of Directors. They expect their spouse to fulfil all their needs. And that's just not fair to your spouse or your business.

## LESSON #58

You can use other people to provide what you need. For example...

... I like to shop and my husband likes baseball. But if I had to drag him shopping with me or if I had to go to baseball games with him — we would both be miserable.

So I go shopping with my friends. And he watches the game alone or with his friends. And we're both happy!

My lesson learned is this: Don't expect your spouse to fulfil all your needs. That's why you have friends. They can fill voids. You can't be all things to your mate at all times.

So I started treating my family and friends as members of my Carline Anglade-Cole Board of Directors. Who do I go to for advice on raising kids? Who can I tap into for solutions to business problems? Who can help me when my husband is driving me nuts? Who can I call just to laugh and have fun with?

I don't expect one of my friends to fill all those needs. My friends are at different ages and at different stages — so I tap into the one who is the most experienced for that issue. I harness their strengths. This saves me time and gives me great insight.

This approach works well for my friends too. Why? Because I'm not burdening them with problems they're not equipped to help me with. I'm not wasting their time and I'm not stressing them out either.

You may already do this subconsciously — but if not — do it now. Create your Board of Directors for your Life company. Empower them to give you direction and advice when asked. Trust that they are looking out for your best interest.

And thank them regularly for being on your team.

## LESSON #59

### A STORY CAN REACH THE HEART AND OPEN THE WALLET.

If I said to you right now, "Once upon a time... "

... amazing things start to happen in your brain!

Neurons... hormones... and synapses trigger activities to prepare for what's about to come next.

Yes — your brain knows a STORY is going to unfold!

Pretty cool, huh?

And it's a powerful lesson to learn — especially if you're a copywriter or marketer!

If you can capture your prospect with a powerful story — you BOOST your chance of creating a killer promo! Why?

Because we're hard-wired for storytelling. Stories reach the heart — and open wallets!

Use this knowledge to your advantage — because stories are gold!

Even in life — some of the funniest experiences start off when someone says, "Let me tell you this story... "

The best way to teach kids a lesson they'll remember is to turn it into a story. Facts don't stick in our brains. Stories do.

Use stories from the Bible... fables... history... and definitely from real life — then watch your copy take on another dimension. You connect... motivate... and become trusted by your reader.

When you tell a story — put your reader right in it! Give enough details so your reader can paint a mental picture. Add facts for credibility. Use a little humor, it's OK. Grab at the emotional heart strings.

When you evoke emotion — you engage your prospect. That emotion can be anger... fear... pain... joy... hope — yep — they can all work to create a compelling story.

Storytelling is another powerful key to my copywriting success. And the formula is simple:

Write an engaging story... connect with the reader... keep the message simple... show why you can be trusted... deliver an amazing offer... ask for the sale. Ka-CHING!

While this formula is very basic — few copywriters follow it. They think it needs to be more "sophisticated" than that. But you don't go wrong when you stick with the basics. And storytelling is a basic approach that is time-tested and proven effective. And the great news is:

Everyone — and every product — has a story. A great copywriter just tells it.

## LESSON #60

### I AM NOT SUPERWOMAN. I JUST PLAY ONE IN LIFE. SOMETIMES I REALLY DO NEED HELP.

People think I have an "S" on my chest.
   They ask me how I do it all...
   How I raised my children...
   How I run a successful business...
   How I have friendships that have lasted over 50 years...
   How I've stayed married for over 38 years...
   And how I've done it all at the same time!
   But let me be the first one to tell you there is no "S" on my chest. If there was — it would stand for "scarred... scared... and soooo tired"!
   I have accomplished great things in my life because I have a lot of help. And I am so thankful for those who help me carry the load.
   How did I raise 4 amazing kids who are genuinely good people? I did not raise my children by myself. I have a wonderful husband who is active and involved in child-rearing. I have a mom and mother-in-law who embraced their roles as grandparents to support me. I had a grandmother (Mama Da) who encouraged and gave me great advice. And I have LOTS

## LESSON #60

of family and friends who stepped into the roles of uncles and aunts. I had a village to raise my kids.

How do I run successful businesses? I have great mentors who taught me valuable lessons that enabled me to launch my businesses. I have colleagues who helped me network and share experiences. I attended seminars and learned from people who are much smarter than me. And I learned from clients — even the bad ones.

How do I keep my marriage strong? With lots of prayer! I have a mate who's committed to our relationship. I have good examples to imitate. I have the Bible and my faith for counsel and direction. And I have the desire to keep working on our relationship — cuz I really do like the guy and I want him in my life forever!

How do I keep my sanity? By recognizing that I am insignificant. By focusing on the REAL life to come. By prayer. By not taking myself seriously. By putting others first. By giving. By being thankful. By realizing that it's all "small stuff" so there's no need to sweat it. By laughing out loud often. By running, I work the machine that is called my body. And by eating Baskin Robbins Praline & Crème ice cream — hence the reason for the running.

So I cringe when someone asks me how I did it all. I didn't. WE did it.

Am I Super? No — but I AM Supported!

\* \* \*

Hey — at the beginning of this book, I promised you 60 kick-butt lessons I learned about copywriting... business... and life — all before I turned 60. But what would a great copywriter do (Lesson #56)?

A great copywriter delivers MORE than promised! So — here are 3 bonus lessons I want to share with you. Why? Because you're special...

\* \* \*

## LESSON #61

### A HANDSHAKE AGREEMENT IS MORE BINDING TO HONEST PEOPLE THAN ANY LAWYER-DRAWN CONTRACT.

Years ago I read the story about Frankie Valli and the Four Seasons. Frankie and Bob Gaudio, the songwriter for the group, were broke teenagers who made a handshake agreement that lasted over 60 years.

They agreed to split their earnings 50-50 for their entire careers no matter what. Well, the rest is history because both men became very successful in their careers — even after they no longer worked together.

They ended up dividing well over $50 million on the strength of that original handshake agreement. They never felt the need to get lawyers involved.

That story BLEW me away!

I love the trust and the respect it shows between two parties who do great work together. And it's a lesson that Clayton Makepeace taught me early in my career.

When I got my first copywriting client, I immediately called Clayton and said, "Help! I got a client but I don't have a contract! Can I use yours as a model?"

I was expecting a document at least a dozen pages long, full of complicated details covering all the possible situations that might come up.

Nope!

Clayton sent me a Word document that took up half a page.

When I asked him about it, his answer was simple: "The contract is just a reminder of what we've already agreed. Does it cover everything? Absolutely not. But it's coming from a place of honesty about what you've committed to do."

So I used that "contract" and I continue to use this same "contract" today — 22 years and many millions of dollars in copywriting packages later.

You can spend a ton of energy drawing up a contract that tries to cover every single thing that could happen or go wrong in the course of a project.

But no matter how hard you try, there will always be a loophole.

If you have to rely on a contract to determine how you're going to handle a situation or a conflict — then you probably shouldn't work with the client.

There needs to be a level of trust, honesty and fairness on both sides.

If you or your client wants to get out of that contract bad enough — all you have to do is pay lawyers a ton of money and they'll figure a way out for you.

So instead of wasting that time and energy — keep it simple. Honor the proverbial handshake agreement you made when you signed up for the project.

Write down what you agreed to do. Write down the payment terms. Write down what happens if the project gets killed at various points. Then get the job done.

Now — I've had large clients who require me to sign attorney-drawn 30-page convoluted contracts. For the most part, as long as they're not asking me to sign my life away, I may agree to sign it.

But if we have a problem — I don't rush to see what the contract says. I pick up the phone and try to work it out with them. And I'm pretty sure they would do the same thing with me.

I have no desire to make lawyers rich because I can't work out a problem with a client.

There have been difficulties in the past with projects but in 22 years as a freelance copywriter, I've never had to get lawyers involved. Yes, I have terminated clients. And I have walked away from money rightfully owed to me. And I don't regret those decisions.

Once clients show they can't honor a handshake agreement — there's no need to continue the relationship.

## LESSON #62

### PUT YOUR PRIDE ASIDE AND TEST, TEST, TEST!

Direct-response marketing makes you humble.

That's because no matter how smart you think you are...

... no matter how much "experience" you have in your market...

... and no matter how great a track record you have...

... the truth is: You really don't know what's going to work! Your market is not static. It's always moving — and you gotta stay on the pulse of it! How do you do that?

Get out of your own way. Stop thinking you're an expert. Present your prospect with a variety of options. In other words...

... you've got to test... Test... TEST!

Test headlines. Test subject lines. Test covers. Test leads. Test offers. TEST!

Then let the market decide what it wants. That's how you get bigger winners FASTER!

True story: I gave a client 2 covers to test for his product. He decided to go with one test cover because he said the other one won't work — it was too BASIC.

## LESSON #62

I said, "How do you know it won't work?" He said he'd been in this business for so long, he just knew it wouldn't work.

I said "OK, well, I like this headline and if you don't want it, I'm going to give it to another client." He said "Fine, OK — but it won't work."

So I gave the headline to the other client who agreed to test it. And guess what?

It kicked butt!

I mean it REALLY KICKED BUTT. In fact — it was the client's BEST headline cover in 2021!

So here's the lesson I learned very early in my copywriting career:

As the copywriter — my job is to create a variety of entry points into the copy. So I write headlines and covers that look very different from each other. I use intrigue... shock... 'how to'... scientific proof... testimonials... and many other types of approaches to snag my reader's attention. Then I get out of my own way. I give my clients 3... 5... or more headlines and covers to test.

And then — it's all about the market! I let the market decide what it wants. And you know what? As long as the market picks ONE of my headlines — then I'm a WINNER!

It doesn't matter if I liked one idea over the other. In fact, most of the time — the cover I'm the most in love with is the one that doesn't work. And vice versa. The cover I don't like most often surprises me and beats the pants off the other ones! Go figure!

Remember: Your role as a direct-response copywriter is NOT to be "creative" — it's to make the sale. And to do that, I remember what my boss Bob King taught me in Lesson #53: Treat your market like a spoiled child. Find out what it wants — and give it to 'em!

That's how you reach A-List copywriter status.

## LESSON #63

### MOVEMENT BEATS MEDITATION.

Just get started. Do something.

Movement beats meditation. Even if it's the wrong thing — it's better than doing nothing at all. You can make corrections along the way.

Most of us overthink stuff WAY TOO MUCH! That's how you develop "analysis paralysis". You keep waiting for more info... research... and insight to make a decision — and nothing gets done.

You hold on to that sales copy after it's final. Why? Because you think a "better" idea will come up. Or it needs just a few more tweaks. This is actually a form of procrastination that can put you out of business and wipe out your savings account.

Turn that copy in. Make a decision. And move on.

I've learned that very few decisions are life-or-death matters. Mistakes are part of the process. They actually help you grow far faster than constant success. Fixing errors is how you learn and heal.

Very few marketing decisions are irreversible. That's why we test. Expect to be wrong more often than right. Remember

— in this direct-response marketing world — a 1% response means you're a success. In other words, 99% of the market will say NO — and you're still a winner!

Those are great odds. They're liberating. It's OK to fail — as long as you fail forward. Learn from your mistakes. Keep trying. Don't give up.

Make a decision... make a plan... and make it happen!

## A SPECIAL GIFT FOR YOU!

### (Actually — you get 14 gifts — and they're worth $1,799!)

Don't you feel like we've bonded? I sure do! So — I'm just not ready to say goodbye yet.

I really appreciate your decision to purchase *Your Copy Sucks — You Don't!* — and to read this book to the very end. I sure hope we can continue this relationship. And I'd like to help you reach your goals — whether it's in copywriting... business... or life! So I want to give you 14 special gifts — worth $1,799 — absolutely FREE!

I chose these gifts because they tie in nicely to the three areas we discussed in this book. And I'm very confident you'll find them valuable if you're an aspiring or working copywriter...

... If you're trying to start or grow a business...

... or if you just need a lil' extra help to make good decisions so you can create the life you desire!

So please accept these gifts from me to you:

**Free Gifts #1, #2 and #3: "Your Copy Sucks — You Don't" Live Critiques! — a $1,200 value — Yours FREE!**

There's a reason why I make my copy cubs repeat the "Your Copy Sucks — You Don't" mantra (in Lesson #34) before I start to crit their copy.

It's because I can be brutal!

But hey — it's my job to find weak spots in your copy — so you can strengthen it and get a winner!

While the process may be painful — the results are worth it! After my crits — many writers go on to deliver killer copy to their clients and get controls!

So do you want to see what it's like to get crits from me? Now you can!

I've got not 1... not 2... but 3 REAL critiques to show you how I work with my writers. You get to watch and learn how you can strengthen YOUR next sales letter.

**In critique #1** — I break down a landing page sales copy and help the writer get a 122% lift in response!

**For critique #2** — I expose big mistakes most writers make when writing bullets — and show how you can avoid them like the plague!

**And in critique #3** — I dissect an email promo — taking it from mediocre to sizzling hot — and show you how to grab your prospect by the eyeballs!

Let me warn you right now: These critiques can get intense! But boy-oh-boy will you learn from them!

And yes — even though we do have FUN — the end result is the same: STRONGER, POWERFUL sales copy that deliver results!

To access **"Your Copy Sucks — You Don't" Live Critiques** — worth $1,200 — just go to https://carlinecole.

com/60-lesson-gifts/

**Free Gifts #4 through #13: All-Star Swipe File! — A $500 value — Yours FREE!**

You get my TOP 10 sales promos that KICK butt! Some are classics that successfully launched products and made my clients tens of millions of dollars!

Study these swipe files! Use them to spark your creative juices — so you can create your own killer promo!

Why am I giving away this vault of valuable sales promos?

First of all: Because I want to!

Copywriting has given me an amazing career. And if you're serious about this craft — it can give you a life you never thought you could have. But to be successful — you've got to learn how to write killer copy!

When you study winning sales copy — you can strengthen your copy skills!

So consider this "paying it forward"! I want the next generation of copywriters to learn and succeed. And you can become a stronger... confident... and IN-DEMAND writer — when you imitate success!

What's more...

... I want to continue the generosity that was shown to me by my mentor, the legendary Clayton Makepeace (Lesson #38). If he hadn't taken the time to teach me and allow me to study HIS swipe files — I would not be the writer that I am today!

In this All-Star Swipe File — you get winning sales copy on blood pressure... anti-aging... vision... sleep... pain... blood circulation... energy... oral health... and much, much more!

Treat this swipe file of my 10 KILLER Sales Promos like a college-level class.

Study the headlines... leads... sidebars... and close. How can you make your copy stronger by using my techniques? It's all there for you to learn — so practice... Practice... PRACTICE! And enjoy this gift from me to you!

To access this **All-Star Swipe File** — worth $500 — just go to https://carlinecole.com/60-lesson-gifts/

## Free Gift #14: An Engaging...Eye-Opening...and Educational Mother-Daughter Conversation on Copywriting... Business... and Life! — A $99 value — Yours FREE!

As a parent — it's easy to assume your children know your struggles. But how can they — if you don't share those valuable lessons with them?

That's a powerful lesson I learned recently. Quite frankly — I was floored that my daughter #2 — fellow copywriter Tiara Cole — had no idea of the "Inner Hustle" it took to succeed in the white male-dominated copywriting world. In fact...

... she knew very little of the struggle of her grandmother and great-grandmother. That's when I had to get to work — and school this kid on her amazing legacy!

Fortunately — this entire event was caught on camera — and shared in an amazing program called "Closing the Success Gap" — led by fellow copywriter Marcella Allison.

Marcella is also the founder of the Mentoress Collective — a forum that provides opportunities for women to network and succeed in business.

During this live interview — with me and daughter #2 — you'll gain insight... knowledge... experience... and even a few "aha" moments to help you succeed in business... family... and life!

Plus you'll witness a hilarious mother-daughter "smackdown" as I teach my youngin' a thing or two about unleashing your "inner hustle"!

After watching this special event — I promise you'll come away with a sense of clarity and direction to help you raise your children and help them succeed.

And when you do — please share your "aha" moment with me! Email me at carline@carlinecole.com. Tell me a lesson learned that made a powerful impact on your life. I'd love to hear about it.

To access **An Engaging... Eye-Opening... and Educational Mother-Daughter Conversation on Copywriting... Business... and LIFE!** — A $99 value — just go to https://carlinecole.com/60-lesson-gifts/

So take advantage of these 14 amazing gifts to give you a winning edge in copywriting... business... and life!

## A BLATANT ATTEMPT TO MARKET AND SELF-PROMOTE!

### (Hey — it's in my nature! I'm a copywriter — that's what I do!)

I'm a direct-response copywriter. My job is to share with you amazing opportunities to help you in copywriting... business... and life! So — how could I NOT tell you about these awesome opportunities available to aspiring and experienced copywriters?

I wouldn't be doing my job — if I didn't share this knowledge with you!

So if you want to boost your copywriting skills... get FREE video training on copywriting... or work with me in an incredible copywriting mentoring program — where you can earn while you learn — then please keep reading...

So you want to be a copywriter –
but you're short on time... cash... and energy?
I can teach you this valuable skill when the kids are asleep...
after you get off work... or on a Sunday afternoon...

# "Give Me 60 Seconds – and I Can Help BOOST Your Copywriting Skills!"

Yes – in just 60 seconds – I can teach you a powerful copywriting lesson to help you write strong headlines... powerful leads... or killer bullets!

Just 60 seconds – and you'll discover winning copywriting secrets that helped my career SOAR to "Million-Dollar Copywriter" status!

And in just 60 seconds – you can grab some powerful tips... tricks... and secrets to write WINNING sales copy! But wait – there's MORE...

...if you got **6 minutes or more** to WATCH and LEARN – I promise to:

- ✔ **REVEAL** "Trade Secrets" to turn you into a copywriting pro!
- ✔ **SHOW** you how to pick winning headlines!
- ✔ **GRANT** you access to the copywriting secrets from elite, A-List copywriters and marketers!
- ✔ **TAKE** you with me on my C.R.A.Z.Y copywriting adventures!
- ✔ **And so much MORE!**

I've got over 200 Copywriting Training Videos that will help rev up your skills – ready to show you – absolutely **FREE**! Just go to my **Carline Cole** YouTube channel and subscribe!

My training videos are available **24 hours a day/7 days a week!** And new videos are uploaded weekly! So if you're serious about becoming a copywriter or just want to BOOST your skills – check out my KICK-BUTT training videos! They're AWESOME... FUN... and my **FREE** gift to you!

## Go to **YouTube.com** and subscribe to my channel: Carline Cole – TODAY!

*Carline Anglade-Cole's Million-Dollar copywriting secrets delivered right to your email – FREE!*

# Get a DAILY Boost of Copywriting Tips... Tricks... and Kick-Butt Strategies to REV UP your Skills!

Join my *CopyStar* Tribe today – and watch your copywriting skills soar! When you're a *CopyStar* – you get access to my proven strategies that give weak copy the muscle it needs to BEAT a control!

I give you 30+ years of my C.R.A.Z.Y copy secrets that keep me on the A-List as an IN DEMAND copywriter! And...

...I teach you how to use my secrets to REV UP your copywriting – and marketing skills too!

Plus – I show you what's working RIGHT NOW in the copywriting industry – to keep you on track and focused on your goals!

If you write **sales letters... email campaigns... long-form copy... Facebook ads... video sales letters... special reports... ezines** – or *any type of sales copy...*

...then you'll love the C.R.A.Z.Y... out-of-the-box... and creative ideas I deliver in every issue of *CopyStar!*

And you get ALL this valuable copywriting and marketing know-how – **absolutely FREE!** Just go to my website: **www.carlinecole.com** – and sign-up for my *CopyStar* ezine today!

## Be a *CopyStar* today!
FREE Membership! ◆ Cancel Any time! ◆ No obligation!

Go to ***www.carlinecole.com*** and sign-up on my homepage!

# How a Mixed-Race Woman Stumbled Into a White Male Dominated Industry – and Kicked Butt!

Let me take you on a journey from my humble beginnings as a Haitian immigrant and stay-at-home mom – to rising to the ranks of a Million-Dollar Copywriter in the highly competitive direct-response industry!

*My Life as a 50+ Year-Old White Male:* How a Mixed-Race Woman Stumbled Into Direct-Response Copywriting and Succeeded! – a 2X award-winner and Amazon Best-Seller – gives it to you straight: The good... bad... and the ugly!

It's brutally honest... guaranteed to give you "AHA" moments... and filled with zany antics that will have you on the floor cracking up!

But most importantly – this book will challenge... coach... and empower you to use your superpowers to create the kick-butt life and career you desire.

Claim your copy today and get $959.83 worth of my Copywriting Swipe File sales promos – **absolutely FREE!** That's 17 winning promos – including my famous "Oprah" launch promo – to inspire you to create your next killer control!

Available in paperback... e-book... audiobook and hardback at
**Amazon.com... Barnesandnoble.com...** and **Kobo.com**

Or you can...

1. Go to **www.carlinecole.com.**
2. Click **"Get My Books"**
3. Select **"My Life as a 50+ Year-Old White Male"**!